BUACHAILLE ETIVE MOR
From Altnafeadh.

Frontispiece

THE SCOTTISH
MOUNTAINEERING CLUB GUIDE

THE
CENTRAL HIGHLANDS

EDITED BY
H. MACROBERT

WITH 49 PHOTOGRAPHS, 15 LINE DIAGRAMS AND A SKETCH MAP

PUBLISHED BY
THE SCOTTISH MOUNTAINEERING CLUB
SYNOD HALL, EDINBURGH
1952

First Edition 1934
Second Edition 1952

CONTENTS

ILLUSTRATIONS

ILLUSTRATIONS—*continued.*

LINE DIAGRAMS

FOREWORD

IN presenting this second edition of the Central Highlands Guide, it should be explained that owing to the Guide Book Committee's decision to issue separate Rock Climbing Guides to Glencoe and to Ben Nevis, a slight re-arrangement of areas has been made. A new Guide Book, " Lochaber," will be issued to include the Mamores, the Ben Nevis group, the Aonachs and the Grey Corries as far as Loch Treig. It is thought that this new Guide Book will be more suitable for climbers from Fort William, the Charles Inglis Clark Memorial Hut and from Steall Cottage. At the same time the Central Highlands Guide continues to comprise the Mamores, Càrn Mòr Dearg, the Aonachs and the Grey Corries, as formerly, as these groups cannot be divorced from a Guide to this area.

Since the first edition of this Guide was issued in 1934, so many new rock climbs have been made in the Glencoe area that it was decided to issue a detailed rock-climbing Guide to that district in a smaller and more portable form, and this has been done. In this second edition of the Central Highlands, accordingly, only the principal rock climbs and the more historical routes have been given in detail, while the new climbs, many of which are extremely difficult, have only been briefly summarised and the reader is referred to the Club's, Guide Book " Rock Climbs in Glencoe and Ardgour," by W. H. Murray, for fuller details.

R. M. GALL INGLIS
General Editor

INTRODUCTION

THE Scottish Mountaineering Club's Guide to the Central Highlands includes the very picturesque and mountainous track of country extending from Ben Cruachan in the south-west to the Monadh Liadth, near Aviemore, in the north-east but excluding Ben Nevis. The boundaries on the north are Loch Linnhe and the Great Glen, and on the south the Oban railway to Dalmally and then a line through Loch Tulla, Loch Rannoch, and Loch Garry to the Inverness railway at Dalnaspidal. Ben Nevis, with its wonderful line of porphyry cliffs, is dealt with in the Club's Lochaber Guide.

The Central Highlands Guide embraces Sections 4, 5, and 6 of Munro's Tables published in the General Guide. These sections comprise 139 mountains over 3000 feet, 70 of which are classed as separate mountains or " Munros." These separate mountains are distinguished in the lists at the beginning of each chapter by being shown in black type. In addition, several mountains under 3000 feet have been included on account of their outstanding position or specially interesting features.

The only map of real use in mountaineering in Scotland is the one-inch Ordnance Survey. The latest edition is the " Popular Edition," 1929, with 50-foot contours but no hill-shading or " layering " ; the older map, with hill-shading and contours, gave a very much better idea of the country. The sheets of the Popular Edition which cover the area dealt with in this Guide are Nos. 42, 43, 47, 48, 54 and 55. The sheets of the old edition, which for some districts are more conveniently cut, are 45, 53, 54, 63 and 64. For fuller details regarding the Ordnance Survey maps, the General Guide should be consulted.

With regard to tracks and foot-bridges over streams, while the latest information available has been given, it must be remembered that a winter's storm may destroy a bridge or completely wash out a hill track.

A most interesting memorandum on the geology of the mountains of the " Central Highlands " has been prepared

1

by Dr. J. Phemister of H.M. Geological Survey, and forms Chapter I of this Guide.

Apart from the mountains, the most outstanding features in this section are the Moor of Rannoch, Loch Awe and the Pass of Brander, Glencoe, Glen Nevis, and the Parallel Roads of Glen Roy. All of these, with the exception of the first, have been referred to in their proper sequence in the Guide. The Moor of Rannoch, forming as it does one of the principal boundaries of the section, does not fit in to any, but has been included in the chapter on Glencoe.

The order in which the mountains have been described, and the groups into which they have been divided, follow on the lines laid down in Munro's Tables. Each group has a separate chapter devoted to it.

The descriptions of the rock-climbs have been made as short as possible, and all minor details excluded. The aim has been to indicate the start of the route, the general line to be followed, and the outstanding difficulties to be met with. Throughout the descriptions " right " and " left " are used to indicate the right hand or the left hand of the climber when facing the mountain.

The Editor would like to express here his great indebtedness to Mr W. H. Murray for his help in connection with the numerous new rock climbs which have been discovered since the first edition of this Guide was published in 1934.

For fuller information regarding any particular mountain or for details of the rock-climbs, the volumes of the *Scottish Mountaineering Club Journal* and the Club's Rock Climbing Guide to Glencoe and Ardgour should be consulted. There is a fully detailed index of the first twenty volumes published separately in two parts. In the *Journal* of the Cairngorm Club, Aberdeen, will also be found many interesting articles on the hills in this section. The more important are :

" The Ridges of Glen Nevis," by E. M. Corner, vol. ii, p. 383.

" Across Creag Meaghaidh," by A. I. McConnochie, vol. iii, p. 232.

" Ben Alder," by W. Garden, vol. iii, p. 261.

" Loch Treig and its Neighbourhood," by T. F. Jamieson, vol. v, p. 1.

" In Cor Arder," by Rev. T. Sinton, vol. v, p. 1.

" The Corryairick and Minikaig Passes," by H. Kellas and
J. G. Kyd, vol. viii, p. 44.

" The Moor of Rannoch," by A. I. McConnochie, vol. xii,
p. 70.

Among other books of general interest relating to the
district embraced in this section the following may be
mentioned :—

Nether Lochaber and *Twixt Ben Nevis and Glencoe*, by the
Rev. Alex. Stewart.

Dorothy Wordsworth's *Tour in Scotland*, A.D. 1803.

Lord Cockburn's *Circuit Journeys*.

The fullest and most authoritative account of General
Wade's Corrieyairack road and other military roads constructed after General Wade's death in 1748 (*e.g.*, the Glencoe
road) is to be found in two most interesting papers by the
late Sir Kenneth S. Mackenzie, Bart., of Gairloch, in the
Transactions of the Inverness Scientific Society, vol. v, pp.
145 and 364.

In Allardyce's *Historical Papers* (New Spalding Club),
vol. ii, will be found a series of Highland Reports, 1749-50,
referring to the military occupation of Lochaber, Glencoe,
and Rannoch after the '45.

The spelling of the Gaelic names of the mountains follows
that adopted in Munro's Tables ; otherwise the Gaelic spelling
agrees with the Popular Edition of the one-inch Ordnance
Survey.   The Gaelic word " coire " or " choire "—both
pronounced " corrie " — is used in conjunction with Gaelic
names.   When the word is used by itself or in conjunction
with the English corruption of the Gaelic it is written " corrie."

Wherever possible translations of the Gaelic names of
the mountains have been given.   In this connection the word
Aonach is of interest.   To anyone well acquainted with the
form and outline of our Scottish mountains, it is obvious
that this name so commonly applied denotes a *ridge*.   Yet
the present-day Gaelic scholars seem unanimous in refusing
this meaning to the word and suggest " meadow," or in
some cases " high ground."

With regard to the photographs, it is regretted that it
has been found impossible to illustrate some of the districts.

MEMORANDUM ON THE GEOLOGY OF THE MOUNTAINS OF THE "CENTRAL HIGHLANDS."

By Dr. J. PHEMISTER of H.M. Geological Survey.

MOST of the mountains dealt with in this *Guide* are composed of the metamorphic rocks (gneisses and schists) which build so much of the Highlands of Scotland. A considerable number are, however, composed of granite and a few, in restricted areas, of lavas and volcanic ashes of Old Red Sandstone Age. From the Monadh Liadth south by Creag Meaghaidh and Drumochter to Ben Alder and Loch Ossian the hills are formed mainly of flaggy gneisses and mica-schist, while granite is distributed over this area in a number of comparatively small masses, for example in the Monadh Liadth (Geal-chàrn Mòr and Beag) and between Loch Ossian and the River Spean. From Loch Ericht, by the Blackmount, to Ben Cruachan, however, granite prevails ; flaggy gneisses, quartzites, and mica-schists appearing again to the east in Glen Orchy. The junction of gneiss and granite crosses the top of Stob Ghabhar, and runs S.S.W. close to the watershed on the east side of Glen Kinglass. This great expanse of granite stretching from Cruachan to Loch Ericht does not constitute one great mass, but is divisible into three units, which are all of Old Red Sandstone Age though the granite of the Moor of Rannoch is relatively the oldest. The other two together form the great outcrop extending from Cruachan to Glen Etive. The youngest, known as the Starav Granite, is a coarse, porphyritic pink rock, splendid for climbing and occupies the centre of the outcrop astride Upper Loch Etive. The granite of intermediate age, the Cruachan Granite, a poor climbing-rock, is medium to coarse in grain, generally grey in colour though pink at the higher levels, and contains a larger proportion of dark minerals than the Starav Granite. It forms a girdle round the latter everywhere except for a couple of miles south of Loch Dochard. This annular or arcuate arrangement of rocks is found again in Ben Nevis and in the Royal Forest. The

4

geological structure of the Royal Forest is of great interest. The summits of Aonach Eagach and of Bidean nam Bian, and the mountains Stob Coire nan Lochan, Beinn Fhada, and Buachaille Etive Mòr and Beag are all built of lavas (" porphyrite ") and volcanic ashes of Old Red Sandstone Age which, resting partly on schist and gneiss, partly on granite, occupy the greater part of an elliptical outcrop, 9 miles long in a N.W. to S.E. direction and 5 miles across. This outcrop is bounded by a curving fracture, known to geologists as the Glencoe Boundary Fault, within which the volcanic pile on its floor of schists subsided into a cauldron of granite magma. The annular fracture runs by Gleann Fhaolinn, Loch Achtriochtan, Meall Dearg, Stob Mhic Mhartuin to Meall a' Bhùiridh. Between Clachlet and Dalness its course is interrupted by the northern end of the Cruachan Granite which invaded the sunken lava-block, and is exposed now beneath the lavas at Buachaille Etive Mòr and in Glen Etive and builds Clachlet and Beinn Mhic Chasgaig. During the subsidence of the lava-block magma rose along the fracture and formed a vertical shell which is known as the Glencoe Fault-intrusion. This shell is usually quite narrow, but at An t-Sròn and Meall Dearg (Aonach Eagach) it widens to form comparatively large outcrops of fine-grained pink or grey granitoid rock.

Many different rocks are involved in complicated geological structure north and south of Loch Leven, but granite, quartzite, and mica-schist form the higher hills ; for example, . Sgòrr Dhonuill and Mullach nan Coirean are of granite, Sgòrr Dhearg and the Pap of Glencoe of quartzite, Beinn na Caillich of mica-schist.

North-eastwards, the Mamore Forest and the Loch Treig hills are composed of mica-schist, quartzite, and flaggy-banded gneisses which run in belts with a N.E. to S.W. direction. The high summits are generally built of the resistant quartzite, for example, Sgùrr a' Mhaim, Am Bodach, Binnein Mòr, Stob Choire Claurigh, Stob Bàn, and both mountains named Stob Coire Easain. Two of the highest hills, however, are formed of mica-schist, namely, Aonach Beag and Stob a' Choire Mheadhoin. The latter lies towards the north end of a mica-schist belt, stretching from the Treig to the Leven, which contains a band of very handsome rock, known as the " Ermine Rock " on account of its characteristic speckling by large black crystals of biotite (black mica).

In the Ben Nevis massif the annular type of structure observed in Glencoe and at Loch Etive appears again. A central area, fully a square mile in extent, of Old Red Sandstone lavas and volcanic ashes resting on phyllites forms the summit of the Ben and is surrounded by fine-grained granite which builds the encircling peaks. An outer shell of grey porphyritic granite, with a larger proportion of dark minerals than is found in the inner granite, girdles the latter on the west, north, and east and reaches its highest elevation on Aonach Mor.

II

BEN CRUACHAN

THIS group lies to the north of Loch Awe and covers some 20 square miles of ground. It is mainly composed of a coarse diorite and stretches east and west in one long line of about 4 miles, sending out two legs of unequal length to the south. The lower slopes are well covered with soil and in many places wooded, but near the tops smooth slabs of granite are exposed, especially round the western tops. The chief summits in the range are as follows :—

(1) **Ben Cruachan** (3689 feet) = properly Cruachan Beann, the mountain of peaks (8 peaks). Between Loch Awe and Loch Etive.
(2) Stob Dearg (3611) feet) = the red peak. ½ mile W.N.W. of (1).
(3) Meall Cuanail (3004 feet) = seaward-looking hill (doubtful). ½ mile S. of (1).
(4) Drochaid Glas (3312 feet) = the grey bridge. 1 mile E. of (1).
(5) **Stob Diamh** (3272 feet) = the peak of the stags. ¾ mile E. by N. of (4).
(6) Stob Garbh (3215 feet) = the rough peak. ⅓ mile S. of (5).
(7) Beinn a' Bhùiridh (2936 feet) = hill of roaring (stags). 1 mile S. of (6).
(8) Sròn an Isean (3163 feet) = the nose of the young bird (chick). ⅓ mile E. by N. of (5).

Ben Cruachan is one of the best known mountains in Scotland. It is one of the few honoured with a place in the schoolboy's geographical text-book ; it appears in Scottish history and in Scottish song ; it is always sure of considerable attention in popular tourist guides to Scotland.

The mountain has many literary and historical associations. Barbour in the fourteenth century writing his history of the Bruce says :

" On other half ane mountain was,
Sa cumrous he, and ek sa stay,
That it was hard to pass that way :
Crechanben hieht that montane
I trow that nocht in all Bretane
Ane hear hill may fundin be."

Pennant in his *Tours*, 1769, refers to the Ben, and states " that it towers to a great height, its sides are shagged with wood and its name means a great heap."

7

In the *Old Statistical Account*, 1793, occur the following passages :—

" The hills are mostly covered with grass ; the most remarkable Cruachan Bean one of the highest mountains in Scotland, thirteen or fourteen miles in circumference, affording excellent pasturage for black cattle and sheep. The sea-pink grows upon it and sea-shells have been found on the summit. Its perpendicular height is said to be 1130 yards above the level of the sea. On the summit of this mountain was that fatal spring and from which according to the tradition of our fathers issued forth the beautiful and extensive lake of Aw."

Macculloch in 1811 was the first traveller to record an ascent. He went up from Taynuilt and found the climb tedious but not difficult.

In 1824 Thomas Wilkinson in his *Tours to the British Mountains* gives rather a quaint description of the mountain :

" Its base is ten or twelve miles in diameter. On the side towards Glenorchy it is concave ; on that towards Lorn it rises with a bold convexity to a great height. By its appearance from beneath there is something of a plain up two-thirds of its ascent ; it then rises with another high hill that terminates in a peak, so that it seems a mountain placed upon a mountain, but I found on further inspection that it has two lofty pyramids, so that its crown is forked . . . from its colour it seems to have little grass upon it, and in some of its deep cavities are lodged snows of former years. . . . For elevation, magnitude and magnificence, I do not recollect a mountain superior to Cruachan."

Botanically Ben Cruachan is not rich, and thus differs greatly from Ben Lui on the other side of the valley, where the rarest plants and ferns are found.

The Pass of Brander, where the River Awe cuts a narrow passage between the steep sides of Cruachan on the north and Creag an Aonaidh on the south, was the scene of two fiercely fought battles in the days of Wallace and Bruce. The exploits of Sir William Wallace here rest on the not very reliable testimony of " Blind Harry," but there seems no

Stob
Dearg
→

Cruachan
→

Drochaid
Ghlas
→

Beinn a'
Chcchuil
→

Beinn
Eunaich
→

A. D. S. Macpherson

BEN CRUACHAN
From Inverinan, Loch Awe,

BEN CRUACHAN MAIN TOP AND STOB DEARG FROM DROCHAID GLAS

doubt that King Robert the Bruce had a great personal triumph here in 1308 against the men of Argyll under John, son of Allastir MacDougall, Lord of Lorn. It is commonly supposed that it was in this fight that the famous Brooch of Lorn was torn from the King's plaid by the MacDougalls, but it would appear that the brooch was actually lost at the battle of Dal-righ near Tyndrum in 1306.

The islands of Loch Awe are also of great historical interest. Fraoch Eilean has the old Castle of MacNaughton, built in the thirteenth century, and Inishail has the ruins of ecclesiastical buildings, tomb, and cross. Kilchurn Castle is an outstanding feature in the views from this district. It stands on a rocky platform projecting from a long, low, marshy peninsula at the north-east end of the loch. It dates probably from 1432, in which year Sir Colin Campbell received the charter of the lands of Glenorchy. It was rebuilt and enlarged about 1615, and was the chief seat of the Breadalbane Campbells until they removed to Taymouth Castle about 1750. It is certainly one of the finest castle ruins in the country. Wordsworth addressed the following lines to the old castle after a visit in 1803 :—

> " Child of loud-throated War ! the mountain stream
> Roars in thy hearing ; but thy hour of rest
> Is come and thou art silent in thy age."

The usual route of approach to Ben Cruachan is by the Falls of Cruachan, about 3 miles along the Taynuilt road from Loch Awe Station. Trains can sometimes be stopped at the Falls Station. The way lies up a well-marked path on the right bank of the stream, and climbs very steeply for some 900 feet. About one mile from the road the lip of the corrie is reached at a height of 1150 feet. The lip is formed by quite a distinct ridge coming down on the right from Beinn a' Bhùiridh. This point is a useful landmark in misty weather. Beyond the lip the corrie is very flat and marshy for ¾ mile, and this portion should be avoided by keeping to the higher ground on either side.

Coire Cruachan can also be reached from Loch Awe Station by a more interesting route which contours up and round the flanks of Beinn a' Bhùridh and circles round into the corrie at about 1000 feet. This route, which is not always easy to follow, branches off the main road a little beyond the

church, and is at first a drove road gradually diminishing to
a sheep track.

To reach Cruachan from the corrie the route goes slightly
to the left, ascending gradually until one reaches the burn
coming down from the Cuanail-Cruachan col. This is followed
to the col at a height of 2700 feet. Thereafter easy slopes
lead to the highest point, 3689 feet. The top is well defined
with a small cairn. The ridge to Stob Dearg for the first few
yards is the same as to Meall Cuanail. It then goes west to
the saddle. It is easily followed by keeping to the edge of
the steep northern slopes. The east ridge to Drochaid Glas
is at first narrow and steep, and may easily be missed in bad
weather, and a descent made either to the south into Coire
Cruachan or to the north into Coire Caorach. The north
ridge is not steep except for the first few feet, but it is a fine
narrow ridge, and forms the best route to the top from
Glen Noe.

From Taynuilt, Cruachan is usually climbed by way of
Stob Dearg, but a direct route to the top is up the Allt
Brander. It is not always easy to pick out these streams
from below, as they fall over very steep ground from a quite
uniform skyline. The Allt Brander, however, forms a small
delta just where Loch Awe gradually becomes the River
Awe. On the far side also a useful landmark is an old wooden
pier. The route goes up the right bank of the stream and
then bears north-east to the Cuanail-Cruachan col. The
main ridge can also be reached direct, between Stob Dearg
and Cruachan, but this route may not be easy when snow
masks the great granite slabs which run across this face.

Meall Cuanail (3004 feet) can be reached easily by both
of the above routes, and this top is usually taken on the way
to or from Cruachan.

Stob Dearg (3611 feet) is the very shapely top seen from
the Taynuilt direction. It is often referred to as the " Taynuilt
Peak." The best route from Taynuilt is by the Allt Cruiniche,
which comes down about ½ mile east of Bridge of Awe. The
stream should be followed to the upper corrie and the summit
reached by the S.S.W. ridge. On the N.W. and N. the
mountain is protected by great slabs of reddish granite,
which give fair rock-scrambling in summer conditions.
Under snow and ice very difficult climbing may be had here,

and one strong party in the early days of the Club (March 1892) took 8 hours on the north ridge. The south-east ridge running to the main top is quite easy.

Drochaid Glas (3312 feet) is usually climbed either on the way to or from Cruachan. In coming east from Cruachan the ridge swings round to the north to reach the narrow rocky top of the Grey Bridge. In mist the climber may easily miss the main ridge at this point, as it really disappears entirely, and the route eastward to Stob Diamh (*pron.* Daff) lies down a steep slope of screes and boulders. Many parties have carried on over Drochaid Glas (on which there is no cairn) and found themselves descending the steep, narrow ridge into Glen Noe. To reach Stob Diamh one should descend to the east, 20 yards short of the top of Drochaid Glas. The north ridge of Drochaid Glas gives a good scramble of 200 feet. The east face has been descended by gullies and ledges, but the rock-climbing is not satisfactory.

Stob Diamh (3272 feet) has been ranked as a separate mountain in view of its distance from Cruachan, and to the fact that it is the meeting-place of three main ridges. It is the highest point of the well-known " horseshoe " of Cruachan as viewed from Dalmally. On its eastern ridge lies

Sròn an Isean (3163 feet), separated from the higher top by a drop of 300 feet. On the south ridge lies

FIG. 1.—Ben Cruachan from the South.
2. Stob Dearg ; 1. Ben Cruachan ; 3. Meall Cuanail ; 4. Drochaid Glas ; 6. Stob Diamh ; 7. Stob Garbh ; 8. Beinn a' Bhùiridh.

Stob Garbh (3215 feet), separated by a drop of only 250 feet. This top is not named on either map, and " Stob Garbh " is a local name. About 500 yards farther south there is a point marked 3091 on the one-inch map, from which the

south horn of the horseshoe runs out east. This " 3091 "
top does not rise more than a few feet above the ridge, but
it is quite prominent from below.

Stob Diamh and the other two tops are usually ascended
in making the circuit of the horseshoe. Coming from Loch
Awe Station a solitary house is passed about ¾ mile along the
Dalmally road, and then on the left a track will be seen
going north across the moor. This is the old railway line
to the disused lead mines, and affords fairly good going for
nearly two miles round into Coire Ghlais. The stream from
this corrie can be crossed by a bridge just above its junction
with the Allt Coire Chreachainn at a height of 503 feet, and
the ridge leading up to the point 3091 followed to the main
ridge. The descent from Stob Diamh to Sròn an Isean is
steep at first, and might easily be missed in bad weather.
The ridge over the Sròn is good going, but the final descent
over the actual nose is very steep grass. The stream should
be crossed and the old railway track followed to the road.

Beinn a' Bhùiridh (2936 feet) is the southern top of the
ridge running south from Stob Diamh. Its grassy and wooded
slopes rise steeply above Loch Awe, and for those who like
to start their climb from the hotel without any preliminary
walking, it forms an excellent route to Ben Cruachan. The
route goes straight up behind Loch Awe Hotel and makes
for the ridge just to the west of the eastern shoulder Monadh
Drisaig (2098 feet). The ridge is then followed to the large
flat top. The descent of the 500 feet to the bealach is quite
steep, and under winter conditions is often icy. The pass
over this saddle is called the Larig Torran (2430 feet). It is
said that Sir William Wallace, in the battle of 1298, surprised
and defeated the men of Lorn by sending his archers and
lightly armed troops over this pass to take the enemy on
the flank and rear.

The north face of Beinn a' Bhùiridh overlooking the Allt
Coire Ghlais is rocky and seamed by gullies, but the only
definite climb here is on the lower crags on the north slopes
of Monadh Drisaig. About ½ mile upstream from the bridge
over the Allt Coire Ghlas a big bluff of rock stands out well
from the hillside. To the left (east) of this there is a short
length of cliff cut out by two well-defined gullies. Between
these gullies is a crack or chimney. This is the climb. The

first attempt was made in March 1891 by J. H. Gibson and R. A. Robertson in very wintry conditions. They reached about half-way up the second pitch. It was attempted again by J. H. Bell and J. Napier in January 1897. It was finally climbed by W. A. Morrison, T. E. Goodeve and A. E. Robertson in January 1905. The first pitch is very wet, but half-way up a good stance will be found in a small cauldron. Then follows easy grass to the second pitch. This starts up a good chimney easy for 15 feet, at which point a difficult traverse to the right is made, followed higher up by an awkward block which has to be got round. Another short grassy stretch leads to the third and final pitch. This pitch is short, and the leader can be assisted by a shoulder from the second man.

Some rock-scrambling can also be had on the north face of Stob Diamh and on the east face of Stob Garbh in Coire Chreachainn.

Glen Noe.—The steep northern slopes of the main east and west ridge of Cruachan fall into the rather remote Glen Noe. The River Noe rises on the saddle between Sròn an Isean and Beinn a' Chochuill at a height of 1800 feet, and flows for 4 miles north of west to Loch Etive. At the foot of the glen is Glennoe Farm, and from here a track leads down the loch to the River Awe, which is crossed by ferry to Bonawe. It is by this route that the fine north face of the Taynuilt Peak is reached, and also the north ridge of the main top. The north faces of the more easterly peaks are usually reached by crossing into the upper part of Glen Noe by the Larig Noe over the saddle from the Allt Mhoille.

EXPOSTULATION WITH CRUACHAN

By the late Professor W. P. KER

Of Crechanben the crewilté,
The driftis dreich, the hichtis hie,
It sair wald tene my tong to tell ;
Quha suld reherss thy painis fell
Forgaitheris with the frenesie.

With fensom feiris thou art forfairn,
Ay yowland lyk ane busteous bairn ;
With mauchie mistis thy mirth is marrit,
With skowland skyis thy spreit is skarrit,
And seitis ar cauld upon thy cairn.

Quhair is thy lown illuminat air,
Thy fre fassoun, thy foirheid fair ?
Quhair is thy peirles pulchritude ?
Quhy stayis thou nocht as anis thou stude ?
Quhy girnis and greitis thou evirmair ?

Return agane fra drowpand dule !
Restoir thy pure wayfarand fule,
And lat him se thee quhair thou smylis,
With Mul, Arane, and the Owt-Ylis,
Into the lufsom licht of Yule.

III

BEINN EUNAICH GROUP

THESE hills form a small group north-east of Ben Cruachan, from which they are separated by Glen Noe and the Allt Mhoille, through which glens runs the Larig Noe from Glen Strae to Loch Etive.

The principal summits are :

(1) **Beinn Eunaich** (3242 feet) = Fowling Peak. 3½ miles N. by E. of Loch Awe Hotel.

(2) Meall Copagach (2656 feet) = the hill abounding in dockans. 1½ miles N.E. of (1).

(3) Beinn Lurachain (2346 feet) = the beautiful mountain. ¾ mile E. of (2).

(4) **Beinn a' Chochuill** (3215 feet) = the peak of the hood. 1¼ miles W. of (1).

(5) Aonach Breac (2935 feet) = the speckled height. 1 mile W.N.W. of (4).

The rocks comprising these hills are mainly Cruachan granite, and a large belt of porphyry occurs on Beinn Eunaich on the south-east shoulder. There appears also to be the usual gneisses and schists interspersed.

Beinn Eunaich (3242 feet) is the dominating mountain of the group, and is well seen from Loch Awe. The usual route is by the easy south ridge, the prominent nose of which is named Stob Maol (1455 feet). To reach this ridge the road to the Castles Farm just under the Stob should be taken. It branches off from the Dalmally road just east of the Allt Mhoille. The nose of Stob Maol is very steep, and gentler slopes may be found round to the east. Thereafter a gradual ascent up a broad ridge leads to the point marked "3174." This is not a top, but merely the junction of two very indeterminate ridges. Two hundred yards farther north is the cairn.

The north-east ridge to Meall Copagach descends steeply for about 600 feet. The west ridge to Beinn a' Chochuill descends less steeply for nearly 900 feet. On the east are steep rocks and gullies, but the only climb recorded here was by D. Scott and R. Anderson in February 1946. From the lowest part of the rocks in the north-east corrie, under snow

15

and ice, a route partly in the gully and partly on a rib of rock was worked out leading to the summit ridge about 15 yards north of the cairn.

The Black Shoot.—The only good rock-climbing is to be found on the outcrop of porphyry on the south-east ridge of Beinn Eunaich. Here is to be found the well-known Black Shoot, the comparatively unknown White Shoot, and the recently discovered Beaver Buttress.

These climbs are all situated on a bold projecting buttress ¾ mile E.S.E. of the summit cairn, and clearly indicated on the one-inch map.

To reach this buttress the main road should be left by a track just to the west of the bridge over the Strae, about 2 miles from Loch Awe Hotel. Just before reaching a very prominent pyramid-shaped moraine and about ¾ mile from the main road the path branches, the left-hand branch cutting diagonally uphill to the left, then dropping slightly to a tributary stream and following this up to the saddle between Meall Copagach and Beinn Lurachain. This left-hand path is followed for another ¾ mile, and then up on the left will be noticed the buttress. The Black Shoot is farther round, and does not come into view until one has rounded the lower ridge and come directly below it.

This was one of the earliest climbs attacked by the Club, and vols. i and ii of the *Journal* tell of three unsuccessful attempts before the final conquest in May 1892. The climbers concerned in these attacks were J. H. Gibson, W. R. Lester, Fraser Campbell, W. W. Naismith, G. Thomson and W. Douglas.

The climb begins at a height of 1750 feet up a " somewhat ill-defined water-slide, a mossy luzula-bedecked wall of very considerable steepness." This can be avoided by climbing the buttress on the right, up a narrow ledge to the left round a delicate balance corner, and then up 40 feet until one can traverse into the Shoot above the water-slide. An easy 20 feet in the gully leads to a little pitch covered with green slimy moss which can be climbed on the left wall. Above this easy ground leads to a deep cleft just below the " Twisted Chimney." This overhangs slightly and gives 15 feet of hard work. About 20 feet up the leader can " jam " himself and bring up the second man. Another 10 feet leads to a

GLAS BHEINN MHÓR AND BEN STARAV FROM STOB COIR' AN ALBANNAICH

April 1925

J. R. Young

THE BEN STARAV GROUP FROM LOCH TULLA

Beinn nan Aighean is between the trees. The dome is Glas Bheinn Mhòr, with Starav to left. The peak is Stob Coir' an Albannaich with the flat-topped Meall nan Eun to right of the nearer Meall an Araich.

large ledge where the party can all assemble. Three obvious routes appear above the ledge, but so far only the direct one leading to a sloping ledge on the right wall has " gone." This part requires caution, and may in certain conditions be found very difficult. Above this easy scrambling leads to the top. The climb is about 300 feet.

The White Shoot is an easier gully to the right, and does not appear to be often climbed. It was climbed in March 1891 by J. H. Gibson, Fraser Campbell, Lester, and R. A. Robertson. About 200 feet up the climbers traversed into an adjacent gully to the right, and finished the climb up a fine chimney.

The Beaver Buttress was first climbed in December 1927 by J. H. B. Bell, Corbett, Parry, and A. P. A. Robertson. The buttress lies to the right of the Black Shoot, and the party had started on the buttress with the intention of traversing into the Shoot above the water-slide. The route was by narrow rock-ledges, which eventually brought the party to a point about 300 feet up overlooking the gully on the right (the White Shoot). Then followed a traverse to the left and two very difficult 15-foot pitches, which would probably be difficult even under summer conditions. Above this, easier rocks led to the summit of the buttress.

To the south of the Black Shoot buttress there is a very conspicuous deep-cut gully. This, however, is mostly grass and scree and affords no climbing.

Meall Copagach (2656 feet) shows up well from Glen Strae. Between it and Beinn Eunaich there is an unnamed top over 2750 feet. The ridge connecting the three is narrow and well defined. It continues east and drops to 2100 feet at the saddle, over which runs the path from Glen Strae to the road in Glen Kinglass (see p. 16).

Beinn Lurachain (2346 feet) rises on the east side of this pass, and with its twin hill **Beinn Mhic-Monaidh** (2602 feet) on the east bank of the Strae form a pair of very conspicuous sentinels for this beautiful glen. The latter especially, with its symmetrical cone, is well known to all climbers in the Dalmally and Loch Awe district.

Although only 2602 feet, Beinn Mhic-Monaidh rises as high above the Strae as Cairn Toul (4241 feet) rises above the River Dee. It can most easily be reached from the Bridge

of Orchy-Dalmally road.   The bridge at the farm Larig no
longer exists, and the farm is empty.   There is a bridge (locked
gate) 1½ miles farther down, south of the Allt-Broigleachan.

Beinn a' Chochuill (3215 feet) is the highest point in a
long, well-defined ridge which runs a little north of west
for more than 4 miles from Beinn Eunaich to Loch Etive.
The usual route to Beinn a' Chochuill from Dalmally or
Loch Awe is by the old railway track (see p. 12) and up the
Allt Mhoille to the bealach at the head of the glen about
1800 feet.   From here 1400 feet of steep grass and scree lead
to the summit ridge.   The mountain is often climbed from
Beinn Eunaich.   The Eunaich-Chochuill saddle is about
2300 feet, and from here the ridge rises steeply to a shoulder
at 2800 feet.   Beyond this the ridge rises gently for ¾ mile
to the cairn.   The ridge leading south by west to the Larig
Noe is not well defined, but there is a quite well-defined little
corrie here just under the summit facing S.E.   The slopes
to the north are very steep but not precipitous.

The long westerly ridge can be followed over **Aonach
Breac** (2395 feet) to A'Chruach above Loch Etive, and the
path taken along the loch to Bonawe and Taynuilt.   There
is a ferry over the River Awe.

IV

BEN STARAV GROUP

THE mountains of this group are mainly granite hills, with steep grassy slopes on the south and west sides, while the north and east sides are bold and craggy and sometimes precipitous. They lie between Loch Etive on the west and the upper waters of Glen Kinglass and Glen Dochard on the east.

The principal tops are as follows :—

(1) **Beinn nan Aighean** (3141 feet) = hill of the hinds. 8 miles W. of Inveroran Inn, Loch Tulla.

(2) **Ben Starav** (3541 feet) = meaning obscure. 1¾ miles S. by E. of Loch Etive Head.

(3) Meall Cruidh (3049 feet) = rounded hill of the shoe. ¾ mile S. by E. of (2).

(4) Stob Coire Dheirg (3372 feet) = peak of the red corrie. ½ mile E. of (2).

(5) **Glas Bheinn Mhòr** (3258 feet) = the great grey hill. 1¾ miles E. of (2).

(6) **Stob Coir' an Albannaich** (3425 feet) = peak of the corrie of the Scotsman. 1⅛ miles N.E. of (5).

(7) **Meall nan Eun** (3039 feet) = rounded hill of the birds. 1½ miles E. by N. of (6).

Beinn nan Aighean (3141 feet) is a very remote mountain, and as it has neither great height nor distinctive features, it is very seldom climbed. The name is spelled " Aighenan " in the new edition of the one-inch map. The easiest route of approach is from the east from Inveroran Inn on Loch Tulla. A private road leads from the Victoria Bridge over the Dochard on the old Glencoe road, ½ mile north of the Inn, right up Glen Dochard and south-west down Glen Kinglass to Loch Etive, passing *en route* the shooting-lodge of Doire-nan-saor. From this road any of the ridges or streams may be followed to the summit.

The route from Loch Awe or Dalmally is up the Lurachain path (see p. 17), over the saddle (2100 feet), and down to the Kinglass. Instead of fording the river in a direct line with the summit, one should continue upstream about one mile and cross at the bridge near the Lodge. When the river is low it is perhaps better to ford it, and go up the left bank of the Allt Hallater by a path which will be of great assistance in climbing the lower steep slopes.

The ridge running north by west drops to 2100 feet before rising to meet the main ridge between Ben Starav and Glas Bheinn Mhòr.

Ben Starav (3541 feet). — This is a very fine peak rising steeply from the head of Loch Etive. It is a big, bulky mountain with a beautifully formed small top. It radiates ridges in all directions, S.W., N.W., N., E., and S.E., five in all, and as they approach the summit they are narrow, and under snow conditions beautifully corniced. Ben Starav is usually climbed from Loch Etive head. There is a motoring road down Glen Etive from the Glencoe road, and the car can be left opposite Coileitir Farm, where there is a bridge across the Etive. From here the north ridge is reached by the bridge across the Allt Mheuran, and leads easily to the summit.

Ben Starav can also be approached by long tramps from Inveroran in the east, by Glen Dochard and the upper waters of the Kinglass, and from Loch Awe in the south by the Lurachain path (see p. 17), and the path up the left bank of the Allt Hallater.

Meall Cruidh (3049 feet) is not marked on the one-inch map, but is indicated in the hill-shaded map by a lump on the south-east ridge just after it turns south. This ridge slopes gently down and swings west, to end in Stob an Duine Ruaidh (2624 feet), the peak of the red man.

Stob Coire Dheirg (3372 feet).—The main easterly ridge of Starav runs at first for 300 yards south-east to the head of the very fine S.E. corrie. It then turns north-east, and in about ⅓ mile rises to Stob Coire Dheirg. This last portion of the ridge is narrow, and sometimes forms a beautiful snow *arête*. The ridge then runs E.S.E. and drops to about 2600 feet, where the ridge from Beinn nan Aighean comes in from the south. It then rises gradually to

Glas Bheinn Mhòr (3258 feet).—This hill is well seen from Glen Etive, rising dome-shaped from its east and west ridges. It is easily approached from Coileitir Farm up the Allt Mheuran, then by the north ridge, which runs out from the west ridge ¾ mile from the summit. This avoids the steep scree and rocks of the north face. Like Ben Starav, it can also be reached from Glen Dochard.

Stob Coir' an Albannaich (3425 feet).—This is the very prominent peak seen from Loch Tulla, looking up Glen Dochard. The top is the highest point of a long ridge running N.W. and S.E. for about 3 miles. Its south-east spurs, Sròn na h-Iolaire (the nose of the eagle) and Cùil Ghlas (meaning obscure) overlook Loch Dochard, and its north-west shoulder, Beinn Chaorach (hill of the sheep), runs down to Glen Etive. It is best ascended from Coileitir Farm by way of Beinn Chaorach.

The climber proposing to reach Glas Bheinn Mhòr from Albannaich in misty weather would be well advised to study very carefully the contours between the two hills. The route goes first south of west and then east of south before turning south-west to gain the ridge to Glas Bheinn Mhòr.

Meall nan Eun (3039 feet) is a very uninteresting flat-topped mountain, with fairly steep sides except on the north and west. It is usually climbed from Glen Etive or from Glen Dochard. Coming from the former, the Etive, unless very low, should be crossed at Coileitir Farm and the track followed north to the Allt Ceitlein. This stream should then be followed up to its source between Meall Tarsuinn (2871 feet) and Meall nan Eun. To reach Albannaich the ridge should be followed over Tarsuinn and then a course made almost due south, which brings one to the foot of a climb of 1000 feet up the steep north side of Albannaich.

V

STOB GHABHAR AND CLACH LEATHAD

THIS very beautiful range of mountains is usually referred to by climbers as the Blackmount, although the forest of that name also includes the Ben Starav group. These mountains were formerly classed as of metamorphic rock, mostly mica-schists, but they are now, according to the Geological Survey, composed mainly of granite traversed by porphyrite dykes. The Cruachan granite appears to extend to the top of Stob Ghabhar.

The principal summits in the range are as follows :—

(1) **Stob Ghabhar** (3565 feet) = peak of the goats. 3¾ miles N.W. of Inveroran Inn.

(2) Stob a' Bhruaich Lèith (3083 feet) = the peak of the side brae. 1½ miles W. by N. of (1).

(3) Sròn a' Ghearrain (3240 feet) = the nose of the gelding. ⅓ mile W. by N. of (1).

(4) Sròn nan Giubhas (3174 feet) = the nose of the firs. ½ mile N. of (1).

(5) Aonach Eagach (3272 feet) = the notched height. ¼ mile E.S.E. of (1).

(6) **Stob a' Choire Odhair** (3058 feet) = the peak of the dun corrie. 1¾ miles E. by N. of (1).

(7) **Meall a' Bhùiridh** (3636 feet) = the hill of the roaring (stags). 2¾ miles S. by W. of Kingshouse Inn.

(8) **Clach Leathad** (3602 feet) = the stony hill. 1 mile S.W. of (7).

(9) Mam Coire Easain (3506 feet) = the pass of the corrie of water-falls. ½ mile N. of (8).

(10) Crèise (3600 feet) = (meaning obscure). ½ mile N. of (9).

(11) Stob a' Ghlais Choire (3207 feet) = peak of the grey corrie. ½ mile N. of (10).

(12) Sròn na Crèise (2952 feet) = the nose of (meaning obscure). ¼ mile N. of (11).

From Stob Ghabhar in the south to Sròn na Crèise in the north is about 4½ miles, and the traverse of this ridge from Inveroran Inn to Kingshouse Inn has long been one of the classic expeditions of the S.M.C. It takes in seven of the tops mentioned above, viz., Nos. 1 and 4, and 8 to 12, but only in one place does the ridge dip below the 2500-foot contour, at the Bealach Fùar-chathaidh (2320 feet) between the ridge Aonach Mòr and Clach Leathad. The whole range is most picturesquely situated on the western borders of the Moor of Rannoch, and is consequently well seen from the main road crossing the Moor to Glencoe, and from the West Highland Railway running north to Fort William. One of the most striking view-points is from the road pass above Tyndrum. The traveller here is greeted by one of the finest mountain panoramas in Scotland : the broad open strath of Orchy with the peaks of the Blackmount beyond. The sharp peak to the left is Stob Ghabhar, in the centre is Clachlet, and to the right is the great ridge of Meall a' Bhùiridh, running out into the Moor of Rannoch. The nearer views of the range, with Loch Tulla in the foreground, are particularly charming.

Stob Ghabhar (3565 feet) lies to the north-west of Loch Tulla and is most easily approached from Inveroran Inn. The river is crossed by the Victoria Bridge ½ mile north of the Inn, and the private road running up the left bank is followed for almost one mile. Here a path will be noticed running up the Allt Toaig. This path ascends gradually, and contours round the south-west slopes of Beinn Toaig and Stob a' Choire Odhair until nearly at the watershed, when it turns and runs east to the saddle between these two hills. The path should be followed to the 1250-foot contour, and then after crossing the stream a route made direct for the summit up the south-east ridge. The summit ridge is well defined, with steep rocks and scree falling to the great eastern corrie and more gentle slopes to the west.

The main backbone of the mountain runs north over Sròn nan Giubhas, and then north-west along the Aonach Mòr to within one mile of Glen Etive. The west ridge runs for ⅓ mile to Sròn a' Ghearrain, which is only marked by the 3200-foot contour in the one-inch map, and then on for another mile to Stob a' Bhruaich Lèith.

The Upper Couloir of Stob Ghabhar.—Immediately below the cairn in the eastern corrie there is a small, rocky buttress split from top to bottom by a great gully. In summer-time the centre pitch of this gully is a particularly objectionable slimy water-slide of about 100 feet, but under winter conditions the gully gives a very fine snow and ice climb. The first pitch is usually snowed up and easy, but sometimes the rocks are showing, forming a double pitch. If necessary a through route is available. Above this very steep snow leads to the famous ice-pitch, which is usually about 15 to 20 feet of perpendicular ice. If this is surmounted, steep snow leads up to the summit ridge within a few feet of the cairn. If the ice-pitch proves impossible, the rocks on the right can be climbed and a very crazy *arête* reached, which leads either to the upper snows or direct up the higher rocks to the summit.

The first ascent of the Upper Couloir was made in May 1897 by A. E. Maylard and three friends.

To reach the eastern corrie one should use the path already referred to, which leads to the watershed (2240 feet) one mile east of the summit. From here one can contour round into the corrie. Above the Lochan, and somewhat to the right of a direct line to the Upper Couloir and the summit, there is the Lower Couloir running up between some rocky outcrops. This Couloir is quite easy, and leads to the snow-field below the Upper Couloir. The summit ridge can easily be reached from this snow-field by keeping to the right of the summit rocks. The climb from the Lochan by the two couloirs to the summit is 1340 feet, of which the Upper Couloir is about 300 feet.

The main feature of the view from Stob Ghabhar, as from the other peaks of the Blackmount, is the great expanse of the Moor of Rannoch, with its innumerable lochs and lochans. The view across Loch Tulla to the Beinn Dòrain group is also very fine.

Stob a' Bhruaich Lèith (3083 feet) is the western summit of Stob Ghabhar, with which it is connected by a long undulating ridge.

Sròn a' Ghearrain (3240 feet) is the nose which projects south from the above ridge. The actual top, unnamed on the one-inch map, is denoted by a 3200-foot contour, and the name of the nose has been given to this summit. The south-east corrie lying between the Sròn and Stob Ghabhar is very deep cut and impressive.

Sròn nan Giubhas (3174 feet), like the last top, is named from its adjacent nose, in this case the prominent east ridge which separates Corrie Bà on the north from the east corrie of Stob Ghabhar. It is denoted by an unnamed 3150-foot contour. About one mile N.N.W. along Aonach Mòr is a top marked 2839 feet, and from here runs out the ridge to

J. Rennie

STOB GHABHAR

The summit rocks with the Upper Couloir (the arrows show foot of Couloir).

SRÒN NA CREISE

the N.E. connecting the Stob Ghabhar group with the Clachlet group. As stated above, the ridge descends here to 2320 feet at the Bealach Fùar-chathaidh.

Aonach Eagach (3272 feet) is the very fine ridge which runs out east from a point ¼ mile S.E. of the summit of Stob Ghabhar. Neither the height nor the name is given on the one-inch map. The ridge is narrow and rocky.

Stob a' Choire Odhair (3058 feet), and its lower summit Beinn Toaig (2712 feet), lie due east of Stob Ghabhar. The path up the Allt Toaig (see p. 23) is the best route from Inveroran. These hills rise immediately above the old road from Inveroran to Kingshouse, and the Stob shows up as a fine rocky cone when viewed from Bà Bridge.

Meall a' Bhùiridh (3636 feet) is the highest summit of the Clach Leathad, or, as it is usually written, the Clachlet group. It lies to the east of the main ridge, with which it is connected by a ridge which, dropping to 3070 feet at the bealach, loses its ridge formation and abuts against the steep slopes leading up to Mam Coire Easain. The usual line of ascent is from the summit of the old road pass (1454 feet) above Kingshouse. When coming from the other summits of the Clachlet it is not always easy in bad weather to find the route down to the connecting ridge.

Clach Leathad (3602 feet) is the south top of the group, and gives its name to the whole range. It is a fine mountain viewed from the south-east, with the great dark Corrie Bà lying between its ridges and the sharply defined Sròn nan Giubhas. The south-west ridge leads down towards the Bealach Fùar-chathaidh, but while still 1000 feet above the pass it swings round to the west, and the route to the pass leads down steep slopes on the south side of the ridge. The north ridge is broad and flat, and stretches north for nearly two miles to Sròn na Crèise. Clachlet can conveniently be climbed from Bà Bridge on the old Kingshouse road, but it is usually approached over the other summits of the group, or from Stob Ghabhar in the south.

Mam Coire Easain (3506 feet).—This top is not named on the one-inch map, but its height is given. It is directly above and west of the saddle connecting the main ridge with Meall a' Bhùiridh. The name perhaps ought to be applied to this saddle. The top has no real claim to be classed as a

c

separate summit. It is denoted in the one-inch map by a 3500-foot contour, but it is doubtful if it rises more than 20 feet above the level of the ridge. Viewed from the west, the skyline of the ridge runs south from Crèise to the saddle north of Clachlet without any apparent rise. In bad weather this alleged top would be of no assistance in locating the route to Meall a' Bhùiridh.

Crèise (3600 feet).—This top is not named on either map. The height " 3596 " on the one-inch map is 300 yards north of the 3600-foot contour. The actual height is probably just a little over 3600 feet. Crèise as viewed from Kingshouse Inn in spring-time is a fine snow peak, and apparently the highest point on the Clachlet ridge. North of Crèise the main ridge becomes narrower, with rocky outcrops on both sides until it reaches

Stob a' Ghlais Choire (3207 feet).—This fine mountain with its projecting northerly ridge, Sròn na Crèise (2952 feet), presents a bold rocky face to Kingshouse. Under winter conditions especially it more than holds its own with its great rival across Glen Etive, Buachaille Etive Mòr. The best route of ascent is by the north ridge, approximately the right-hand skyline as seen from the Inn. This north

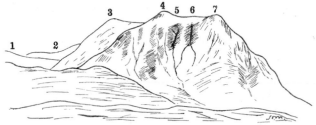

FIG. 2.—Sròn na Crèise.
1. Ridge to Meall a' Bhùiridh ; 2. Clachlet ; 3. Crèise ;
4. Stob a' Ghlais Choire ; 5 and 6. Gully climbs ; 7. Sròn na Crèise.

ridge can be reached from the Glen Etive road by crossing a swing foot-bridge. There are several good buttresses of rock on the ridge, but these can all be avoided by keeping to the right, and no difficulty will be found in reaching the top of the Sròn. From here the easy main ridge leads to Stob a' Ghlais Choire.

A little climbing will be found on the steep easterly face between the Sròn and the Stob. There are two prominent gullies with straight-cut sides running up the centre of this last face. To the left of the more southerly, 5, is a rock buttress more or less in a line with the summit of the Stob. This was climbed in June 1903 by Dr. and Mrs Inglis Clark, and gave a fairly continuous climb on easy rocks.

Gully 5 was climbed in July 1907 by J. Martin. The gully branches half-way up, and the route to the left across the rock buttress was followed. This part gave the best climbing (150 feet), and has one good pitch about 100 feet from the fork.

The buttress to the right between the two gullies was climbed about 1898 by J. S. Napier, but there is no information in regard to it.

Gully 6 is in two portions at foot. These join half-way up and form a deep-cut straight-edged gully very prominent under both winter and summer conditions. The gully was climbed by J. Martin in July 1907, and found to be quite easy, the only interesting part being the deep-cut portion near the top.

Under winter conditions the above routes may all be snowed up, and the only features visible are the rock buttress below the summit, and the deep-cut upper part of Gully 6. The best route to the summit then is probably by the great open snow gully to the left of the rock buttress. This leads to the summit ridge just to the north of the cairn on Stob a' Ghlais Choire.

There are also some rocks in the corrie to the south-east of the Stob. These are about 250 feet high, fairly steep but loose. D. W. Piggott made a route up these rocks direct to the summit and reports that the climbing was of good standard all the way.

On the west side of the Sròn overlooking Glen Etive will be found a small pinnacle not unlike the famous Cioch in Skye.

Formerly the Blackmount was easily accessible from the Inveroran-Kingshouse road. Since the opening of the new road to Glencoe, which crosses the Moor of Rannoch some miles farther to the east, the old road has been closed for traffic between the Victoria Bridge, just north of Inveroran, and the point where the new road crosses the old road about one mile south of Kingshouse. It is hoped that this old route will be preserved as a right-of-way.

VI

GLEN CRERAN HILLS

THESE hills lie to the east of Glen Creran and to the west of Glen Etive. The principal tops are :

(1) **Sgòr na h-Ulaidh** (3258 feet) = the peak of the hid treasure. 3½ miles S. of Clachaig Inn, Glencoe.

(2) Stob an Fhuarain (3160 feet) = the peak of the well. ½ mile N.E. of (1).

(3) **Beinn Fhionnlaidh** (3139 feet) = Finlay's Ben. 1¼ miles S.W. of (1).

(4) **Beinn Sgulaird** (3059 feet) = (meaning obscure). 3 miles E.N.E. of Loch Creran head.

The first two are most easily ascended from Clachaig in Glencoe, and the last two from Glen Creran.

Sgòr na h-Ulaidh (3258 feet) is the highest point of a broad ridge, two miles long. From the summit the ridge goes N.E. to Stob an Fhuarain, then it turns N. and is known as Aonach Dubh a' Ghlinne. West from the summit a short ridge runs out to a shoulder Còrr na Beinne (2982 feet). On the north side of the Sgòr is a steep rocky corrie (Coire Dubh) pierced by a gully from top to bottom, well seen from the north, and now known as the Red Gully.

The usual route of ascent is from Clachaig. Cross the bridge over the Coe at the back of the hotel, and go down the Glencoe road till it crosses the Fionn Ghleann. Follow up the road on the left bank to the keeper's cottage where the steep north end of the ridge is right in front of you. Climb the steep 2000 feet to the ridge and then follow it over several small tops to Stob an Fhuarain, and then S.W. to the main top. There is also a track direct from Clachaig to the cottage, crossing the Fionn Ghleann by a foot-bridge. From Glen Creran the route lies up the road to Salachail and then east up the Caol Creran to Corr na Beinne. If coming north from Beinn Fhionnlaidh by the Bealach Caol Creran (about 1500 feet) two routes offer themselves : one to the left (N.W.) up an easy ridge over Corr na Beinne to the top ; the other, to the right (N.E.), follows a wire fence for about ½ mile to a subsidiary col Bealach Clach nam

Meirleach (a little under 2200 feet), here the fence takes a sharp turn N.W. and lands you within 100 yards of the summit (small cairn). From the last-named bealach the hillside can be skirted to Bealach Fhionnghaill (1914 feet), whence Clachaig can be gained by Fionn Ghleann. On this east side of the hill there is a certain amount of rock, and hands can be used every now and then.

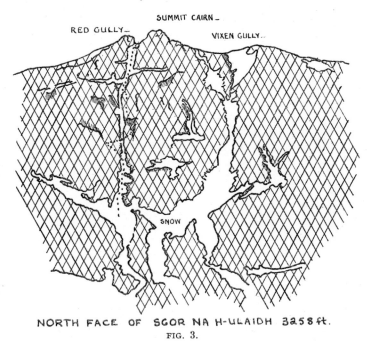

NORTH FACE OF SGOR NA H-ULAIDH 3258 ft.
FIG. 3.

In summer the ridge is perfectly simple; in winter, if the snow be hard, an ice-axe is needed: the descent (some 300 feet east) from the summit is steep and so is the slope to the west. In fact, if time is of importance, the ridge should be followed right down; in any case do not strike west till Stob an Fhuarain is passed, when ordinary grass slopes will be met with. Going north from the Stob a gentle descent is followed by two slight rises before the final descent is commenced.

The Red Gully referred to above as the very conspicuous gully running up the north face of Sgor na h-Ulaidh directly below the summit cairn was finally climbed on 26th February 1950 by Douglas Scott, J. C. Henderson and Rob. Anderson. The climb of approximately 650 feet took just over 6 hours. The gully contains four ice pitches leading to a steep snow slope finishing in a great rock gateway just under the summit. The route follows the gully up two ice pitches. A traverse under the third ice pitch to the right leads on to a narrow rock rib bounding the gully on the west. The crest of this rib is followed until it merges in the final steep snow slope avoiding the fourth ice pitch. In the opinion of the pioneers the Red Gully is one of the major snow and ice climbs in the Glencoe district.

Vixen Gully.—On 14th March 1948, G. Allison and J. G. Black (both J.M.C.S.) and R. Anderson (S.M.C.) descended this gully glissading. A vixen crossed the foot of the gully below them, hence the name.

A gully further to the west, and running down from the Col to Corr na Beinne, was climbed in snow in February 1948 by J. G. Parish, D. H. Haworth and J. S. Berkeley. It gave about 1000 feet of snow with a steep finish of 30 feet of difficult iced rock.

Beinn Fhionnlaidh (3139 feet) (*pron.* Ula) has a rock-strewn plateau ⅜ mile long for a summit, the highest point being the E. end where there is a small cairn. East of the summit for a few yards the ridge is narrow and then there is a sudden drop of some 150 feet, where an ice-axe is needed in winter. The ridge then broadens out again, and ½ mile from the summit a wire fence is struck, which ½ mile farther on, just after passing over a small top (2694 feet), turns north and the ridge descends steeply to Bealach Caol Creran (about 1500 feet)—a descent of 1200 feet in just over ½ mile. Every now and then the fence comes to an end on a perpendicular bluff, and under heavy winter conditions an ice-axe would be essential. In summer it is, of course, an easy scramble. North-west from the summit plateau a small headland juts out named Caoran (2944 feet). On the north side of the summit plateau crags run down into Coire a' Chait, but no definite climb is likely to be found here. On the south side also crags run down into Coireachan Odhar, but these are much more shattered and broken up than those on the north and interesting scrambling can be had.

The best route of ascent is up Glen Creran to Ellerlic, and then east along the side road toward Glenure Farm. From here the long shoulder running out west from the summit to Leac Bharainn should be followed.

A more interesting route, if streams are not in spate, is to reach Glenure Farm by part road part track on the E. side of the Creran, crossing the bridge just below Glasdrum one mile north of the end of Loch Creran. Take the track from the farm on the north bank of the River Ure to the Allt Bealach na h-Innsig, cross this stream and ascend its left bank, making use of deer-tracks, to Lochan na h-Uraich (1000 feet). Continue for another ½ mile and then make north for the crags on the south slopes of the mountain, and have as much or as little scrambling as you like until you reach the plateau not far from the summit.

Beinn Sgulaird (3059 feet) is a fine double-topped hill, well seen by those going from Creagan to Ballachulish *via* Glen Creran, or perhaps even more distinctly from the shores of Loch Etive. Its summit ridge, about 2½ miles, forms roughly the shape of an S running N.E. and S.W. At the south end of the ridge is a nameless top (2807 feet), then a dip to 2597 feet, rising to Meall Garbh (2668 feet), dip to 2579 feet, summit cairn 3059 feet, dip to 2855 feet; second top one-fifth mile from summit (2963 feet), where the ridge divides. The main ridge runs north, then curves east; while the spur runs east, and the two form a semicircle containing Coire nan Tulach facing east. The north ridge is an easy slope running down to a small lochan (2087 feet), above which rises Stob Gaibhre (2244 feet) the end of the ridge. The south ridge of the corrie is steep, and hands are needed for scrambling up and down.

The easiest route of ascent is from Creagan Station along the road on the north side of Loch Creran (3 miles) to the bridge just below Glasdrum. Cross the bridge and carry straight on eastwards to the ridge which runs out west from the southern top (2807 feet).

The descent from the N.E. end of the ridge may be made from Stob Gaibhre to the path on the left bank of the River Ure, and so down to Glenure Farm. The track from here to Glasdrum bridge referred to above is then followed and the main road rejoined.

The mountain may also be climbed from Loch Etive head by the Allt a' Bhiorain, which passes round the north end of Beinn Trilleachan and leads to the head-waters of the Ure. From here the route lies up Stob Gaibhre and along the ridge to the summit. Beinn Trilleachan is a very shapely mountain rising steeply with rocky slopes above Loch Etive and forming with Ben Starav, on the opposite side of the Loch, a most impressive gateway to Glen Etive.

From just south of Salachail (300 feet) at the head of Glen Creran a good track strikes off N. to Ballachulish Station (some 6 miles) *via* Gleann an Fhiodh (col about 1400 feet).

If one wishes to go from Salachail to Clachaig, a nearer way as regards distance, though not necessarily as regards time, is to follow a very rough track from the sheepfold ¼ mile N.E. from Salachail, keeping well above the Allt Eilidh to a newly built reservoir. Cross the stream just before the dam, and keep the east side of the reservoir (if burn is in spate, walk along the dam and take W. side) ; then follow the stream to where it turns south, strike N. of E. over a col (about 1050 feet)—only rough track in places—and follow a stream leading into the Allt na Muidhe. If stream full, keep the left bank from the col. Just north of Gleann-leac-na-muidhe (a keeper's cottage), which stands on the right bank, a bridge crosses the stream and a good road leads thence to the new Glencoe road. A track on the east bank leads more directly to Clachaig, crossing the Fionn Ghleann by a bridge ; from here to the main road at the back of Clachaig Inn the track is poor.

The nearest way from Clachaig to Glen Etive is *via* Fionn Ghleann to its head over Bealach Fhionnghaill (1914 feet) and down by the Allt Charnan to Invercharnan, 3½ miles from the pier at the head of Loch Etive.

Robt. M. Adam

BEINN SGULAIRD

April 1912

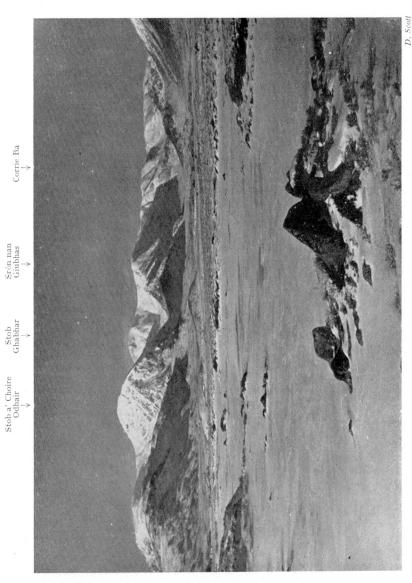

Stob a' Choire Odhair   Stob Ghabhar   Sròn nan Giubhas   Corrie Ba

THE MOOR OF RANNOCH AND THE BLACKMOUNT

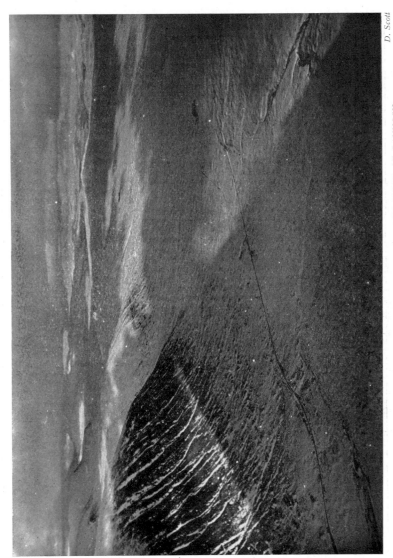

D. Scott

THE SHADOW OF BUACHAILLE ETIVE MOR ON THE MOOR OF RANNOCH

J. R. Young

THE BUACHAILLES OF ETIVE

Looking up Lower Glen Etive to the Lairig Gartain with Stob Dubh on left and Stob na Broige on right,

33

VII

THE BUACHAILLES OF ETIVE
(The Shepherds of Etive)

THIS group of mountains lies in the angle between Glencoe and Glen Etive, and consists of two nearly parallel ridges called the Buachaille Etive Mòr and the Buachaille Etive Beag. The principal summits are as follows :—

THE BUACHAILLE ETIVE MÒR—

(1) **Stob Dearg** (3345 feet)=the red peak. 2¼ miles W. by S. of Kingshouse Inn.

(2) Stob na Doire (3250 feet)=the peak of the copse. 1¼ miles S.W. of (1).

(3) Stob Coire Altruim (3065 feet)=the peak of the nursing corrie (*i.e.* hinds with fawns). ⅝ mile W.S.W. of (2).

(4) Stob na Bròige (3120 feet)=the peak of the shoe. ½ mile S.W. of (3).

THE BUACHAILLE ETIVE BEAG—

(5) **Stob Dubh** (3130 feet)=black peak. 1 mile N.W. of (4).

(6) Stob Coire Raineach (3029 feet)=peak of the corrie of the ferns 1¼ miles N.E. of (5).

(7) Stob nan Cabar (2547 feet)=peak of the antlers. ½ mile N.E. of (6), and 1½ miles W.N.W. of (1).

Stob Dearg, or, as it is commonly called, Buachaille Etive, is always referred to as being in Glencoe. Actually the head-waters of Glencoe only come as far east as the Buachaille Etive Beag, while the River Coupall, a tributary of the Etive, almost completely surrounds the Great Shepherd. By custom, however, the whole valley from the sea at Loch Leven to the Moor of Rannoch is known as Glencoe.

The highest point of the group lies in the apex of the angle between the glens, and the ridge of the Buachaille Etive Mòr runs from it for about 3 miles parallel to Glen Etive. The ridge of the Buachaille Etive Beag lies about 1½ miles to the west. It is separated from the higher ridge by a deep valley, the Lairig Gartain. To the west of the Buachaille Etive Beag there is another deep valley, the Lairig Eilde, through which there is a path from Dalness in Glen Etive to the Study in Glencoe (4 miles, saddle 1650 feet). The whole area now belongs to the National Trust for

Scotland, who also own the Bidean nam Bian Group and the Aonach Eagach in Glencoe.   The whole Trust property, about 13,000 acres, is roughly a triangle with its three points at Dalness Lodge in Glen Etive, Clachaig Inn on the north-west, and Kingshouse Inn on the north-east.   Free and unrestricted access to all the mountains, corries and glens is permitted at all times, and it is the intention of the Trust to preserve this beautiful mountain district in its present wild state and no roads, paths, cairns or signposts will be allowed and no new buildings of any kind may be erected.

Kingshouse Inn, situated just off the new Glencoe road, is the most convenient centre, but, of course, this new road brings Tyndrum Hotel or even Crianlarich on one side, and Ballachulish and Clachaig Inn on the other, within easy motoring distance.   There is also a cottage Lagangarbh, near Altnafeadh, which has been leased to the Club by the National Trust.   It is a well appointed Club Hut with accommodation for about 16.

Stob Dearg is the dominating peak of the group, and is in every respect one of the finest mountains in Scotland. It rises without any intervening minor heights in one steep slope from the great plateau of the Moor of Rannoch.   To the moor it presents a grand cone of broken black rock. The finest views are to be had in the early morning, when the level rays of the sun stretch across the moor and light the eastern face of the mountain.   The most striking features of the view from the summit are the wide expanse of the Moor of Rannoch to the north-east, with the cone of Schichallion showing prominently, and the glimpses of Loch Leven and Loch Linnhe to the west.   The mountain prospect, though very extensive, is somewhat monotonous, as none of the nearer mountains have from this point of view any striking character or shape.   From a rather lower height, for instance from the col between Stob Dearg and Stob na Doire, the Bidean nam Bian group shows a fine bold outline, particularly if silhouetted on the evening sky.

From Stob na Bròige, though much that is seen from the higher peak is lost, a full-length view of Loch Etive is gained.

Any of the peaks of the group may be ascended in almost any direction without serious climbing, except Stob Dearg on its east and north sides.

To ascend Stob Dearg without serious climbing one should follow the Glencoe road for 3 miles, from Kingshouse to Altnafeadh ; cross the Coupall River by a footbridge, and strike up into the corrie opposite (Coire na Tulaich). After a somewhat rough scramble over screes the summit ridge will be reached, about half a mile to the west of the cairn and at a height of 2900 feet. There is no difficulty in following the ridge to the summit. In descending, return to this col, and the route can then be varied by going down on the Glen Etive side by Coire Cloiche Finne, or the walk may be continued over the other peaks of the ridge.

The way down by Coire Cloiche Finne from the summit cairn may easily be missed in bad weather, as it is necessary to go at least 400 yards south-west before starting the descent to Glen Etive. In descending one must continuously bear to the right, otherwise difficult broken and rocky ground will be encountered. Should the ascent be made by Coire Cloiche Finne from Glen Etive, the road down the Glen should be followed for about 2 miles from the new Glencoe road before striking up the steep slopes to the right.

If the walk is continued along the ridge, about $1\frac{1}{2}$ hours from Stob Dearg will be found easy time to reach Stob na Bròige. Another $1\frac{1}{2}$ hours easy going will take one down to the Lairig Gartain (1600 feet) and up again to the summit of Stob Dubh. The descent to Glencoe may then be made along the ridge of Buachaille Etive Beag.

Stob na Doire (3250 feet approx.) is only named on the six-inch map.

Stob Coire Altruim (3065 feet) is a local name for this bold rocky summit. The top has no name on either the one-inch or six-inch map.

Stob na Bròige (3120 feet) is the south-west end of the Buachaille Etive Mòr. Viewed from Loch Etive direction this peak and Stob Dubh present two beautifully symmetrical cones connected by the Bealach Lairig Gartain.

Stob Dubh (3130 feet) is the south-west end and highest peak of the Little Shepherd. The highest point is 150 yards N.N.E. of the point marked 3129 feet on the one-inch map.

Stob Coire Raineach (3029 feet) slopes gently down to its north-earterly nose, **Stob nan Cabar** (2547 feet). This nose is usually referred to as the Buachaille Etive Beag in the same way as its neighbour Stob Dearg is known as the Buachaille Etive Mòr, or more generally as " The Buachaille."

Rock Climbs on Buachaille Etive Mòr

The formidable appearance of the great northern and eastern cliffs of Stob Dearg long protected it, and it was not till March 1894 that a very strong party, Messrs Collie, Solly, and Collier, made the first recorded ascent. Since then many different routes have been found, several of which present no serious difficulty. The face is well broken up, and much variation is possible. The huge rock buttress called the " Crowberry Ridge " in the centre of the north face is the best known climb. The rock is a coarse, reliable rhyolite called " porphyry."

The rocks to the east and south of the Crowberry Ridge as far round as the Chasm are divided vertically by gullies and horizontally by rakes and ledges, so that not more than 250 feet of continuous rock-climbing can be had without reaching a more or less easy escape by way of grassy ledge or gully.

The principal climbs are enumerated below in order, from north-west to south-east, and may be identified from the accompanying diagrams and photographs.

For further details of all the climbing routes the reader is referred to the Club's Rock-climbing Guide to Glencoe and Ardgour by W. H. Murray.

Gully A : The Great Gully.—This gully has been frequently ascended. There is no record of its first ascent. Often in winter it is quite filled up with snow, and becomes a walk. In summer-time it is not so easy. There are some small pitches, and at one place near the foot 100 feet of wet rock garnished with watercresses and other aquatic plants has to be passed. Under thin snow the gully has been found difficult, and might become very difficult. This gully should not be glissaded without actual knowledge of the conditions in its lower section.

Cuneiform Buttress.—This is the small buttress about 350 feet high which lies high up in the Great Gully under the rocks of the North Buttress, from which it is separated by a wicked-looking black chimney known as the Ravens Gully. The buttress was climbed in June 1930 by J. H. B.

J. Rennie

BUACHAILLE ETIVE MOR
From the North (see Fig. 4).

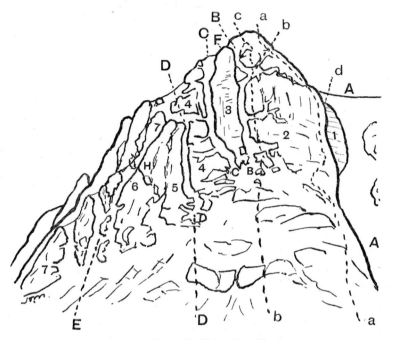

Fig. 4.—Buachaille Etive from North.
A. Great Gully; B. Crowberry Gully; C. Easy Gully; D. D Gully; E. Water-slide Gully; F. Crowberry Tower; H. Heather Ledge. 1. Cuneiform Buttress; 2. North Buttress; 3. Crowberry Ridge; 4. Curved Ridge; 5. D Gully Buttress; 6. Central Buttress; 7. Collie's Climb. a, b, c. Routes on North Buttress; d. Ravens Gully. (For details of routes on 3 and 6 see figs. 5, 7 and 8.)

Bell and Alex. Harrison. Rubbers and scarpetti were used. The route lies to the right or west of two chimneys well seen from below. The climbing is by small ledges and holds which slope outwards. High up a capacious crowberry-covered ledge was reached, and from here all attempts to force a way up direct by the left failed. The route to the right overlooking the Great Gully, however, went easily over excellent rock. Then followed a steep shelf, hardly a chimney, leading up the vertical west face of the buttress. Above this the route turned in to the centre of the face, and a chimney, followed by a wall, landed the party on the summit of the buttress.

Ravens Gully.—This dark rift is very well seen from the road near Altnafeadh. It was first climbed in June 1937 by J. B. Nimlin's party. There are 11 pitches, only one of which is easy. The others are " very difficult " or " very severe in rubbers," and the height is about 450 feet. This is a very fine gully climb.

The North Buttress.—This is the huge rounded buttress on the east of the Great Gully. It was first ascended by Messrs Brown, Rose, and Tough in July 1895. Their route kept close to the gully, and the general line followed is as shown by (*a*). The height is about 1000 feet.

The central portion of the buttress appears to be climbable almost anywhere, but it is always steep and interesting, with chimneys, cracks, and ledges. The very prominent chimney in the centre of the buttress seen from the road is not difficult, and forms one of the many variations possible here.

On the left of the buttress two successive chimneys, or narrow gullies, run up to a conspicuous ledge known as High Ledge which crosses from the Crowberry Gully just above where it forks, to the Great Gully near the top of the Cuneiform Buttress. Between these chimneys and the Crowberry Gully there is quite a well-defined ridge. This was climbed in April 1905 by Newbigging, Morrison, and Burns (*b*). They started from the Crowberry Gully below the first pitch, up a shallow depression above a well-marked rectangular recess. Keeping to the rocks overlooking the Crowberry Gully, they reached High Ledge. Above this an interesting chimney led to the summit. There are about ten other routes between Ravens Gully and the Crowberry Gully, varying from 120 to 400 feet. Two outstanding ones, Guerdon Grooves, climbed by John Cunningham and W. Smith, and Bottleneck Chimney and Hangman's Crack (280 feet), climbed by R. G. Donaldson and G. R. B. Carter, are first-class routes of " very severe " standard. Guerdon Grooves is probably the hardest climb in Glencoe.

The Crowberry Gully.—This magnificent deep-cut gully lies between the North Buttress and the Crowberry Ridge. It has been climbed several times under snow conditions, and its difficulty then varies with the state of the snow or ice, but is not usually less than severe and may be impossible. Under summer conditions it gives a first-rate rock-climb.

It was first climbed without snow in September 1910 by H. Raeburn, F. Greig, D. H. Menzies, and S. F. M. Cumming.

There are eight principal pitches : the sixth pitch is the well-known Thincrack Chimney. It is about 50 feet high. The route goes up the narrow chimney to a window formed by a jammed stone. The chimney is too narrow to permit of back- and knee-work, and progress must be made by shuffling and wriggling. A much-needed rest may be found on the chock-stone. From the stone an awkward step out on the right wall and a pull over a projecting boulder lead to the top of the pitch.

Above this the fork of the gully is reached ; the left fork runs up to the Crowberry Tower gap or neck, and is " very severe " ; the right fork runs up to the easy rocks at the top of the North Buttress.

To reach the right fork it is necessary to climb a difficult little pitch in the Crowberry Neck Gully to a wedged stone. From here a traverse is made to the right into the right-hand or true continuation of the main gully.

An easy stretch then leads to the last formidable pitch— a big cave with high overhanging roof and greasy walls. Like the first pitch this has to be avoided on the right wall. The route goes up to a grassy ledge and round a corner. From here an interesting chimney and good rock lead back again to the gully above the cave. Thereafter a few small easy pitches and some scree lead to the summit. This is one of the finest gully climbs in Scotland, especially under winter conditions.

The Crowberry Ridge.—This very fine narrow rock ridge lies directly under the summit of Buachaille Etive when viewed from the north. It is bounded on the north-west by the deep rift of the Crowberry Gully (B. Gully) and on the south-east by the shallower Easy Gully (C. Gully). These two gullies converge and join below the Crowberry Ridge where the rocks of the Curved Ridge curve round to the north and join the lower rocks of the North Buttress about the 2400-foot contour. The drainage from the two gullies flows over the hard rocks of the junction, forming a water-slide before reaching the highest slopes of heather and scree, where it forms a small ravine. The route to the Crowberry Ridge, the Curved Ridge, and the North Buttress lies up

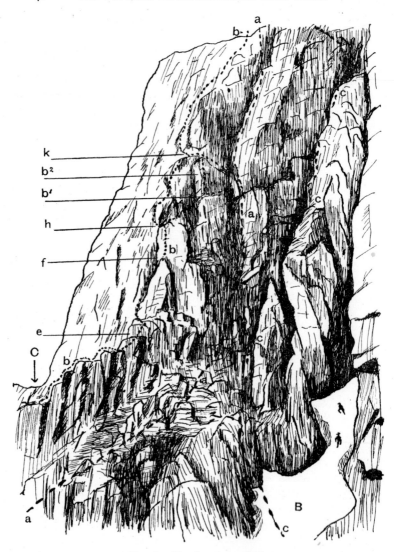

FIG. 5.—The Crowberry Ridge.

B. Snow in Crowberry Gully ; C. Direction of Easy Gully.
a. Naismith's Original Route ; b. Abraham's Direct Route ; b¹.
Greig's Ledge ; b². Speirs's Variation ; c. Shelf Route ; e. Foot of
steep rocks ; f. Top of Pinnacle ; h. Abraham's Ledge ; k. Upper
Ledge.   The Hyphen Rib lies between routes a. and c.
(See also Fig. 7 for diagrammatic sketch of the Ridge).

THE CROWBERRY RIDGE

From the foot of the North Buttress (see Fig. 5).

BUACHAILLE ETIVE MOR
From Kingshouse Inn (see Fig. 6)

L. St. C. Bartholomew

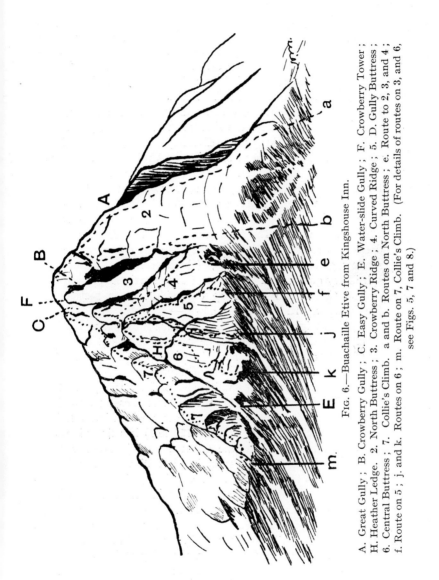

FIG. 6.—Buachaille Etive from Kingshouse Inn.

A. Great Gully ; B. Crowberry Gully ; C. Easy Gully ; E. Water-slide Gully ; F. Crowberry Tower ; H. Heather Ledge. 2. North Buttress ; 3. Crowberry Ridge ; 4. Curved Ridge ; 5. D. Gully Buttress ; 6. Central Buttress ; 7. Collie's Climb. a and b. Routes on North Buttress ; e. Route to 2, 3, and 4 ; f. Route on 5 ; j. and k. Routes on 6 ; m. Route on 7, Collie's Climb. (For details of routes on 3, and 6, see Figs. 5, 7 and 8.)

D

the right bank of this ravine, right up to the rocks where it crosses the foot of the water-slide to the left bank on the lower rocks of the North Buttress. From this point the two ridges and the buttress can be easily reached.

Between the crest of the Crowberry Ridge and the Crowberry Gully there is a subsidiary shallow gully which in its lower part is more of a shelf. This shelf lies alongside the lower rocks of the ridge, which abut against the very steep middle portion. Where the shelf starts to steepen and form a gully a rib of rock appears, dividing the shallow gully into two parts. The left-hand branch goes straight up and then bears slightly to the left. The right-hand part is at first, for about 100 feet, a deep-cut chimney; it then becomes less steep and forms more of a shelf for about 200 feet. This 300-foot stretch is parallel to the very steep middle section of the ridge itself. The formation here is therefore : (1) the deep-cut Crowberry Gully; (2) a deep-cut chimney with a shallow gully or shelf above; (3) the continuation of the subsidiary gully; and (4) the crest of the main ridge.

The three main routes up the middle steep section of the Crowberry Ridge are as follows :—

(1) The original route up the line of the subsidiary gully (a).
(2) The direct route up the crest of the ridge (b).
(3) The route up the line of the deep chimney and the shelf above the Crowberry Gully (c).

All these three routes unite above the steep part at a height of about 2750 feet. Another 250 feet of easy scrambling leads to the foot of the Crowberry Tower, which is the finish of the ridge climb. The Tower (3150 feet) is a fine pinnacle which can be seen from the Glencoe road just below and slightly to the left of the summit. It falls very steeply for about 40 feet to a narrow neck connecting it to the main mass of the mountain. From the neck to the summit cairn is an easy scramble of about 230 feet.

(1) *The Original Route.*—The Crowberry Ridge was first climbed by W. W. Naismith and W. Douglas in August 1896, and described by the former in a charming article in vol. iv of the *S.M.C. Journal.* The pioneers naturally followed the easiest route on the ridge, and consequently climbed by the subsidiary gully or shelf referred to above and then by the left branch of the gully higher up. No serious difficulty was

THE CROWBERRY RIDGE
The left traverse from Abraham's Ledge.

encountered, and the whole climb only took two hours for the 750 feet. The ridge owes its name to the numerous clumps of ripe crowberries found by the party throughout the climb.

(2) *The Direct Route.*—In May 1900 G. D. Abraham, A. P. Abraham, J. W. Puttrell, and E. A. Baker, after careful exploration and prospecting, succeeded in forcing a way directly up the face of the precipitous middle portion, roughly 200 feet, from the 2500 to the 2700-foot contour.

The lowest rocks at 2400 feet can be reached most easily from the foot of the Easy Gully. These lead up to the foot of the perpendicular section (*e*). Here a great pinnacle lies against the face with chimneys on both sides. The east chimney is the route. On the square top of this pinnacle (*f*) a good stance will be found from which to tackle the next pitch, a face climb of 15 feet. The handholds throughout, however, are satisfying, and even in ice and snow this section from (*e*) to Abraham's Ledge (*h*) at the top of the 15-foot pitch should always be climbable.

Arrived on Abraham's Ledge, at first sight it would appear that a cul-de-sac has been reached. There are, however, three routes of escape, one out to the left, one upwards to the right, and the third down a chimney to the right.

The direct route goes to the left, out on to a very exposed face. The only handhold is for the right hand on the edge above the ledge. Standing on very inadequate holds, the right hand relinquishes reluctantly what appears to be the last link with safety and is transferred to a sloping slab breast-high, on to which a hand balance is made. A cautious crawl of a few feet up this slab leads to an open corner up which the route goes on better holds for another 20 feet. Here a good ledge (*k*) is reached about 40 feet above (*h*). This ledge goes round to the right and descends obliquely into the subsidiary gully and joins the original route.

Above platform (*k*) the route goes slightly to the left round a corner and into an open chimney. A climb of 30 feet up this brings the climber on to less steep ground about 2700 feet. The route now goes up over easy slabs and then steep heather and grass to the foot of the Crowberry Tower (3000 feet). The Tower (3150 feet) is climbed on its west side without any difficulty. A descent of 40 feet leads to the grassy col connecting the Tower with the summit rocks. The direct descent to the col is slightly overhanging, but easy routes on very rotten rock will be found both to the right and to the left. The col can be reached direct by traversing the Tower on its west side.

Greig's Ledge Variation.—(b^1) A variation of the direct route can be made so as to avoid the difficult pitch between (h) and (k). The pioneers of this route were F. Greig, E. R. Beard, and R. Adamson in April 1907. The route leads up from the west end of Abraham's Ledge into and across an open corner of rock. The farther wall of this corner terminates in a straight edge of rock on which will be observed the beginning of a good ledge. The only difficulty is getting round the edge on to the ledge. This ledge, Greig's Ledge, leads easily into the subsidiary gully of the original route. A climb of a few feet up the gully leads to another ledge running diagonally up to the left, back on to the crest of the ridge. This ledge leads to platform (k).

The subsidiary gully and this upper ledge can also be reached from platform (f) by traversing round easy ledges or from platform (h) by descending the little chimney referred to above. These are the best routes to take under icy conditions.

Speirs' Direct Variation.—(b^2) In September 1928 a further variation of Greig's route was made by W. B. Speirs, R. R. Elton, and G. R. Speirs.

At the straight edge of rock referred to above, the leader, not liking the look of the traverse round the edge on to Greig's Ledge, climbed directly up the perpendicular edge on very small holds some 20 feet to platform (k). This is a very fine variation of Abraham's original route to the left and equally direct and exposed.

(3) *The Crowberry Shelf Route.*—This lies to the right of the original route. It branches off from the subsidiary gully about the level of platform (e) on the direct route. It was first explored and climbed, all but the last chimney, by H. MacRobert and R. A. Brown in April 1910. At that time the ridge was plastered with snow and ice, and great difficulty was experienced even in traversing from platform (f) into the subsidiary gully. From here the only feasible route appeared to be up the steep shelf or gully to the right as

Naismith's route was an ice-fall. Several hours were spent in reaching the final chimney, the difficulties of which caused a retreat.

In September 1920 it was climbed by Wilding and Pigott, and in May 1923 by Garrick and Biggart. This summer ascent in 1920 was not noted in the *S.M.C. Journal*, and the route has been known since 1923 as Garrick's Shelf.

The first ascent under winter conditions was made in March 1937 by W. M. Mackenzie and W. H. Murray, and found to be " very severe."

Higher up the shelf becomes more of a shallow trough, until it once again steepens and thins down to a scoop lying in an angle between the wall on the left and a small pinnacle rising out of the Crowberry Gully on the right. This is the end of the shelf, and the only exit is up the scoop or open corner which is very difficult. Above this the easy rocks below the Tower are reached.

The Shelf Route may be reached easily from the Pinnacle Ledge (*f*) or from Naismith's Route. It can also be taken direct from below by a deep-cut conspicuous chimney just to the left of the Crowberry Gully traversing to the left wall three-quarters of the way up.

The Hyphen Rib is between the Shelf Route and Naismith's Route, and is the conspicuous rib about 300 feet high, well seen in the photograph (p. 40). It was first climbed in September 1937 by A. C. D. Small and J. R. Wood.

The Crowberry Tower at the top of the Crowberry Ridge is a very imposing pinnacle, especially when viewed from high up on the Curved Ridge. It has been climbed from all sides.

The South Chimney, first climbed by J. H. Bell, J. Napier, and G. Higginbotham in April 1898, is the obvious route from the Curved Ridge or Easy Gully. The route goes straight up the centre of this face by the line of a deep-cut vertical chimney 40 feet high.

This face above Easy Gully is steep, exposed and rather loose. It can be climbed almost anywhere.

There is an easy traverse from the Ridge round to the left below the Tower into the Easy Gully which may be very useful as a quick way of escape in bad weather.

The Fracture Route to the left of the Direct Route is one

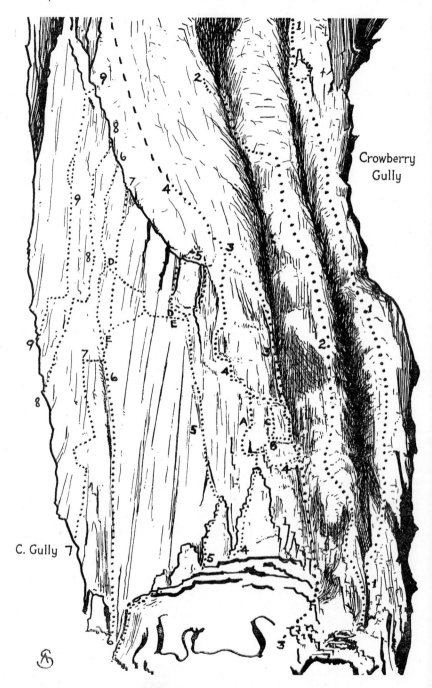

Crowberry
Gully

C. Gully 7

of the best climbs on the Crowberry Ridge. It was climbed in October 1946 by K. Copland and W. Smith. It is a " hard, severe in rubbers," and runs up about 225 feet on the left half of the face in the line of a conspicuous V-cleft, and finishes above the Slabs on the Direct Route.

About two-thirds up it is crossed by the High Level Traverse which leads from the Upper Ledge on the Direct Route across the face to Agag's Groove on the Rannoch Wall.

Rannoch Wall.—This is the easterly flank of the Crowberry Ridge and rises some 200 feet above the Easy Gully. At first sight the face looks smooth and vertical if not actually overhanging. A closer examination shows it to be intersected by grooves, cracks and ledges and although very steep and exposed, it may be said to be climbable almost anywhere by really expert rock climbers.

The first route up it was made in June 1934 by G. C. Williams, G. F. Todd, G. G. Macphee, and I. G. Jack, and is now known as Route 1 (230 feet). It lies on the left-hand or higher part of Rannoch Wall. The second route Agag's Groove (350 feet) was made in August 1936 by J. F. Hamilton, A. Anderson and A. C. D. Small, and lies at the lower end of the Wall. It is the longest climb on the Wall.

There are at present six principal routes and seven variations, most of them ranking as at least " severe." Three of these are excellent routes made by I. H. Ogilvie (*J.M.C.S.*) with Miss Speakman namely Satan's Slit, Red Slab and January Jig-saw, and with R. Frere, Girdle Traverse. Other shorter routes but of " very severe " standard have been worked out by K. Copland, J. Cunningham, C. Lyon and W. Smith.

The Easy Gully (C Gully).—This is the gully between the Crowberry Ridge and the Curved Ridge. Under snow conditions it may be a walk the whole way and has been glissaded by many parties. In summer there are one or two

---

FIG. 7.—Diagrammatic Sketch of Crowberry Ridge.

1. Shelf Route; 2. Hyphen Rib; 3. Original Route; 4. Direct Route; 4(A). Abraham's Traverse; 4(B). Greig's Ledge; 4(C). Speirs' Route; 5. Fracture Route; 5(D). Helical Route; 5(E). High Level Traverse; 6. Agag's Groove; 7. Satan's Slit; 8. Red Slab Route; 9. Rannoch Wall (original or No.1 Route).

pitches which are not quite easy, but they can be avoided by traversing on to the easy rocks of the Curved Ridge. The Easy Gully and the Curved Ridge are often used as a quick route of descent. By the Curved Ridge Kingshouse Inn can be reached from the summit cairn by a fast party in about 1¼ hours, but not under winter conditions.

The Curved Ridge.—This is the easiest of the rock routes on Buachaille Etive. It is, however, quite a long and well-defined ridge running from about the 2100-foot contour to the 3000-foot contour. The lowest rocks are rather slabby and water worn and are not often climbed. The route usually taken starts at the water-slide below the Crowberry Ridge (see p. 39) and follows the crest of the ridge, which at first bears to the left and then runs straight upwards. About half-way up, the ridge degenerates into an easy scramble for about 200 feet, after which it again becomes steeper with some quite interesting rocks. At the top a narrow ridge of grass and scree circles round towards the summit rocks below the Crowberry Tower gap. Under winter conditions the climb may be quite difficult.

As the mountain is cone-shaped all the routes on the north-east and east faces converge towards each other as they ascend. In consequence some parties finish the Curved Ridge by ascending the Crowberry Tower by the South Ridge or Chimney. In the same way climbers coming up the routes farther south, from the Central Buttress or from Collie's Climb, find themselves in misty weather confronted by an imposing tower which eventually proves to be the Crowberry Tower.

D Gully.—This gully is usually just a walk under snow, and it is rather a poor climb in summer. It is a clean-cut regular gully of about 600 feet running straight up between the Curved Ridge and D Gully Buttress.

D Gully Buttress.—This is the narrow buttress immediately to the left or south of D Gully. It shows up well on the photograph facing p. 37, and appears to be the right boundary of the Central Buttress. On the right the buttress falls sharply into D Gully ; on the left it is separated from the Central Buttress by a shallow scoop, which at the foot is a heather and grass gully, and higher up a succession of chimneys. This heather and grass gully bends to the left

J. G. Robinson

THE CHASM
Below the 1st Pitch.

THE CROWBERRY TOWER

Showing the S.E. Ridge, the East Chimney and the Easy Traverse below the Tower
into the Easy Gully (*C*).

W. S. Thomson

RANNOCH WALL

J. Rennie

LOOKING S.E. FROM BIDEAN NAM BIAN

The long ridge of Clachlet, the deep gap of the Bealach Fùar-Chathaidh, Stob a' Choire Odhair, with Beinn an Dothaidh behind, Beinn Dorain behind the long ridge of Aonach Mor, which runs from just above the snow top in the foreground round to Stob Ghabhar on the extreme right.

and cuts across the Central Buttress forming the conspicuous Heather Ledge. The top of the buttress is marked by a cairn which also marks the top of the Central Buttress. Above this cairn is a grassy patch leading to the upper part of the Curved Ridge.

The buttress was first climbed in October 1903 by W. C. Newbigging. This party apparently traversed out of D Gully on to the ridge, thus avoiding the difficult pitches at the foot.

The ridge was again explored in July 1929 by Harrison, Addenbrooke, and Bartholomew. The start is at the lowest rocks below and well to the left of the water-slide under the Curved Ridge. After a very difficult slab, which can be avoided, 150 feet of easy ground followed by 80 feet of scrambling on rough firm rock leads to the crux of the climb, a slab of 60 feet. The rock, however, is superb, although the holds slope out. Above the crux there is another 60 feet of slabs. Thereafter the ridge becomes narrow but easy.

The Central Buttress.—Looking from Kingshouse Inn, a steep buttress of rock appears to fall from the summit of Buachaille Etive and finish on the heather slopes between two conspicuous streams which unite a little lower down. The top part is the Crowberry Tower ; then comes the finish of the Curved Ridge, then the upper portion of the Central Buttress, and lastly, at the foot and separated from the upper portion by a conspicuous heather ledge, the lower portion of the Central Buttress. On the left these buttresses merge more or less into the hill face, but on the right they fall steeply into bounding gullies. Figure 4, from the north, shows their relation to each other clearly. The Central Buttress appears as a gigantic pyramid about 800 feet high, but the northerly edge, as explained above, is D Gully Buttress, and the Central Buttress proper is rectangular shaped. It projects somewhat and has a distinct face to the north. It is cut in half horizontally by the Heather Ledge. It is bounded on the south by the indeterminate gully (E) with a conspicuous water-slide, slightly yellow in tone as seen from Kingshouse. Its lowest rocks are about the 1750-foot contour. The first ascent of the buttress was made in April 1898 by J. H. Bell, Higginbotham, and Napier. They climbed a tongue of rocks and heather to the Heather Ledge. They then traversed along the ledge to the water-

FIG. 8.—Central Buttress.
(Enlarged from Fig. 6.)

D. D Gully; E. Water-slide Gully; H. L. Heather Ledge.
P. Pinnacle on k Route. f. D Gully Buttress Climb; g. Original
Route (1898) on Central Buttress; j. Bell and Harrison's Route
(1929) now North Face Route; k. Allan and Bell's Route (1931)
now Direct Route to H. L. and Central Chimney above; kl.
variation to n; l. Slanting Ledge; n. Spillikin Route; m. Collie's
Route (approx.) and ml. direct variation of route.

slide and a small waterfall, and then turned directly up,
following roughly the upper part of gully E. This route
hardly qualifies as a rock-climb in summer, but under genuine
winter conditions it is the only route so far climbed. The
first direct ascent of the buttress, the north face route, was
made by J. H. B. Bell and A. Harrison in July 1929. They
started up the rocks on the right, which face roughly east
of north. After a difficult 20-foot right-angled corner, some
excellent steep climbing on good rocks landed the climbers

on the Heather Ledge just before it starts to fall steeply to the right to form the boundary line of D Gully Buttress. Above was the upper edge of the buttress, and the route went up to the left and then crossed the edge to the right to a sloping cave. From here it was necessary to traverse downwards to the right where two chimneys were in evidence above. They were now in the shallow scoop with D Gully Buttress immediately on their right. The most direct or left chimney was ascended and found to be overhanging and difficult, necessitating combined tactics on the left wall. Above this, steep and interesting climbing led to the cairn at the top of the buttress, and the climb was completed as usual by the upper rocks of the Curved Ridge. This route above the Heather Ledge is now called the Central Chimney.

In 1936 an improvement was made to the finish of the climb by D. Scott, J. C. Henderson, A. M. McAlpine and W. H. Murray. From a grass platform above the difficult chimney a traverse is made hard to the left on outward sloping holds to a short steep crack and the finish is made up the N.E. edge to the top.

In November 1931 the face of the buttress was ascended from its lowest point by C. M. Allan and J. H. B. Bell. The start of the climb is in the recess above and to the right of the small stream, coming out of the south boundary gully E. The route leads up 190 feet of good steep rock to a small pinnacle sticking out from the face. This is easy to pass on the right. 70 feet above it a grass-covered ledge is reached running up to the right. From here a difficult overhanging crack about 20 feet high leads to easier ground. The crack itself is very exposed. About 40 feet higher the Heather Ledge is reached. This is now known as the Direct Route.

Above the Heather Ledge the upper part of the buttress, about 250 feet high, has three somewhat ill-defined ridges. The right-hand one or most northerly is the edge of the buttress. The central one rises from a large platform on the ledge just to the north of a decided step-up on the ledge. The left one is the narrowest and forms the southern boundary of the buttress.

The route selected for this first ascent, now known as the Central Chimney, was up the central ridge to where it becomes very steep, forming a nose. Here an awkward traverse to the right leads to a steep slab below a long vertical chimney. A good belay between two rocks, one above the other with a recess behind, protects the party while the leader struggles with this very severe chimney. On the first ascent Allan ran out 120 feet of rope before reaching a suitable belay at the top of the chimney. The middle section, about 30 feet, is exceptionally exposed and severe, and here a smooth corner to the right of the chimney is used. At the top there is a conspicuous chock-stone which is, however, easily passed. Beyond this easier rock leads to the cairn at the junction of the buttress with D Gully Buttress.

There are two very fine routes above the Heather Ledge, Slanting Ledge and Spillikin Route. The first starts from the highest part of Heather Ledge and leads up some 40 feet on a heathery ledge running up diagonally to the left. The standard is "very difficult" and the route was made by W. M. McKenzie, J. K. W. Dunn and J. Ewart in May 1937.

The Spillikin Route was first climbed in July 1934 by C. M. Allan, J. H. B. Bell and Miss M. B. Stewart, and the standard is "very severe." The start is from the south end of Heather Ledge up 80 feet of easy rock to a second ledge above which the cliff steepens. The crux of the climb is above this in two pitches of 50 and 15 feet. This is an excellent and very varied climb. The first ascent was made from the Pinnacle P on the Direct Route by a difficult climb straight up to the Heather Ledge.

Collie's Route.—Immediately to the left of the Central Buttress and across the water-slide (E Gully) will be seen a series of small, steep rock buttresses rising one above the other in the direction of the summit cairn. This was the original route up the cliffs of Buachaille Etive, and like many others in Scotland was discovered and climbed by Professor Norman Collie. In his party were also G. A. Solly and J. Collier. In March 1894 they attacked the rocks of the great unclimbed face at what appeared the lowest point. They started up the snow in the gully to the left of their ridge, but almost at once traversed on to the ridge. At the top of the first 250 feet it is necessary, to avoid a sheer 80 foot face, to make a descending traverse into the Water Slide Gully and regain the crest of the buttress above the impasse. The route then continues up in a direct line to the summit.

The lower rocks are good and fairly continuous, but higher up they are more indefinite, and a route could be followed up steep heather and scree avoiding the rocks altogether. At Easter when this route was first followed, it makes a first-rate climb over rocks not too difficult and up steep snow and ice gullies. In June 1939 W. Russell and A. Slack climbed the 80 feet face referred to above, thus straightening out the route.

To the south of Collie's Climb the rocks become very broken up, with heather and scree slopes until the Chasm is reached. There are no defined routes on this part of the mountain, but very amusing scrambling can be had by keeping straight ahead in line for the summit.

An exception is the Lady's Gully immediately to left of Collie's Climb which is a fine gully climb of 800 feet. The lower half was climbed by Mr and Mrs G. D. Abraham in October 1900, and called after Mrs Abraham. The upper half was climbed in November 1946 by W. M. Mackenzie and J. K. W. Dunn. There are about 12 pitches, some of which are " very difficult." The gully forks some 400 feet up and the right fork is the direct line. The left fork starts with a great cave which has only been climbed when banked up with snow. Above the cave there are no further pitches.

Chasm North Wall.—This is the ridge bounding the Chasm on the north. It was first climbed in December 1895 by J. H. Bell, M'Gregor, J. Napier, and R. G. Napier, and called the Four Day Ridge. The route starts about the 1500-foot contour and keeps along the ridge overlooking the Chasm, and is just a scramble in many parts. High up a fine buttress is climbed by means of a gully ending in a long chimney or steeply inclined shelf. The top of this buttress is cut off from the upper part of the ridge by a gap about 50 feet wide with vertical walls. Slightly to the right and 20 feet down an *arête* of rock bridges the gap and abuts against a rib of rock projecting from the other side. The route lies across the *arête* and up the rib of rock to a gully which again ends in an easy chimney. This leads to the upper slopes of the mountain about the 2900-foot contour.

The Chasm.—This is one of the longest and most difficult gully climbs in the country, its only possible rival being the Clachaig Gully (p. 82). It starts at a height of 1220 feet and finishes on the upper slopes of the mountain at a height of 2600 feet.

The foot of the climb is only 20 minutes' walk from the Glen Etive road.   The rock scenery high up is on the most splendid scale.   There are 16 pitches not counting several short easy ones, and the most difficult (" very severe ") are No. 10, Converging Walls Pitch, and No. 15, The Devil's Cauldron.   There are several escape routes available on the south (left) wall.

The Chasm was first named and explored in July 1898 as far as the foot of the 100-foot pitch (No. 8) by J. H. Bell and J. Maclay.   In June 1903 H. Raeburn, Dr. and Mrs Inglis Clark explored and climbed several further pitches and escaped out of the ravine by a steep climb up a pinnacle on the south wall above pitch 12.   This pinnacle gave a good climb of 200 feet.   It was christened the Lady's Pinnacle (2500 feet) and is joined by a little col to the slopes above. The subsidiary gully which comes in here on the south has some good pitches.   In April 1906 H. Raeburn and W. N. Ling with the aid of snow in the gully climbed as high as the Devil's Cauldron.   Here, although one-half of the 150 foot pitch was wiped out by the deep snow, it was impossible to get off the snow on to the rocks owing to the great " randkluft." They managed to force an exit, however, up the south wall and reached the Lady's Pinnacle of 1903.   The next serious attempt was not made until April 1920, when R. F. Stobart, N. Odell, and Mrs Odell succeeded also in reaching the Devil's Cauldron (No. 15).   This party climbed the south wall up a very severe 120-foot chimney.

The Chasm was persistently attacked in 1930 and 1931 by J. G. Robinson, W. B. Spiers, G. F. Todd, R. R. Elton, D. W. Robinson, G. R. Spiers, and I. G. Jack, in various parties, and finally, on 30th August 1931, J. G. Robinson and I. G. Jack reached the Devil's Cauldron in 4 hours, and after a desperate struggle of 3 hours gained the top of the great 150-foot pitch, above which an easy scramble led to the top of the gully.

This completes the account of all the principal routes on the faces of Stob Dearg of Buachaille Etive Mòr from the Great Gully (A) round to the Chasm.

On the lower cliffs to the west of the Great Gully there are three Buttresses with two easy gullies between them. These are Great Gully Buttress, Broad Buttress and Staircase Buttress. The crests of Great Gully Buttress and of Broad Buttress are only rock scrambles, but on the east face of Great Gully Buttress are several fine climbs, some of them " severe." To the west again is the last buttress, Lagangarbh Buttress, at the entrance to Coire na Tulaich. The Lagangarbh Chimney (200 feet) splits the upper part of the Buttress. There are four pitches, the last one of 50 feet is the most difficult. It was first climbed by P. M. Barclay and A. R. Ramsay in September 1930. There are other very difficult climbs on this Buttress.

VIII

BIDEAN NAM BIAN

BIDEAN NAM BIAN is the highest mountain in Argyllshire
and one of the finest mountain groups in all Scotland.
Unfortunately the summits of the group are so steep and
close together that it is impossible to get a proper view of
them except from the top of some more or less distant peak.
From the Mamore summits, for instance, the dominating
feature of all the views is Bidean nam Bian, not even the
Ben Nevis group rivalling it in majesty and beauty of outline.
The northern spurs, however, which overhang the south side
of Glencoe, are most impressive when seen from the Study
at the head of the Glen, but the actual summit of Bidean
itself is so shut off by its outliers that only a glimpse of it
can be had from the Glen, near Clachaig Inn.

The peaks of the Bidean group are as follows :—

(1) **Bidean nam Bian** (3766 feet) = the pinnacle of the hides (cattle
used to fall over the precipices). 1¾ miles S.E. by S. of Clachaig.

(2) Stob Coire Sgreamhach (3497 feet) = the hill of the rocky corrie.
¾ mile S.E. of (1).

(3) Beinn Fhada (3120 feet) = the long hill. ½ mile N.E. of (2).

(4) Beinn Fhada, N.E. top (3064 feet). ¾ mile N.E. of (2).

(5) Stob Coire nan Lochan (3657 feet) = the hill of the corrie of the
little lochs. ½ mile N.N.E. of (1).

(6) Geàrr Aonach (about 2500 feet) = the short height. ¾ mile N.E.
of (5).

(7) Aonach Dubh (2849 feet) = black height. ¾ mile N. of (5).

(8) Stob Coire nam Beith (3621 feet) = hill of the corrie of the birch
trees. ⅓ mile N.W. of (1).

(9) An t-Sròn (about 2750 feet) = the nose. ½ mile N.N.W. of (8).

Bidean nam Bian is usually climbed from the Glencoe
road ½ mile east of Clachaig Inn. The new road crosses the
River Coe here and gives access to the lower slopes of An
t-Sròn. Bearing slightly to the left, the climber should
make for the lip of the corrie where the stream comes out
in a little ravine. Entering the ravine and crossing the burn
the best route goes up the right bank and where the stream
forks (about 1750 feet) turns south-east and goes right up
into Coire nam Beith. The remains of an old deer fence will

Easter 1912

J. H. Buchanan

THE BIDEAN NAM BIAN GROUP

From Aonach Eagach ; Beinn Fhada and Stob Coire Screamhach on left, Stob Coire nan Lochan in centre, with Aonach Dubh below
Bidean just appearing, and Stob Coire nam Beith on right.

(see Fig. 11)

be crossed about 2000 feet, and the simplest route thereafter is to go straight on up the stream, and climb on to the saddle between Bidean and Stob Coire nan Lochan. The ridge from the saddle to the summit is narrow and fairly steep, but except under severe winter conditions is just a walk. In coming down by this route care has to be taken lest the ridges running out to the twin buttresses near the summit be followed by mistake.

The view from the top of Bidean from south round to west is very fine, with the peaks of Cruachan, Loch Etive, the Glen Creran hills, the western ocean, Mull, and the hills of Morven and Ardgour following in succession. The views northward to Nevis and the Mamores, and eastwards over the Moor of Rannoch and to Clachlet are also good. The summit itself with its three supporting ridges is a very perfect mountain form, especially under winter conditions when these ridges are narrow snow *arêtes*.

A very fine ridge walk may be had from An t-Sròn to Beinn Fhada. An t-Sròn is easily climbed from the fork of the stream at 1750 feet, and thereafter it is a delightful ridge walk over Stob Coire nam Beith and a little subsidiary top to Bidean nam Bian. From Bidean the ridge descends at first S.E. then E.S.E. to Stob Coire Sgreamhach. It then turns N.E. to the two tops of Beinn Fhada. The ridge here is fairly narrow, but there is no scrambling. A descent should be made after the N.E. top into Allt Coire Gabhail, now known as the Lost Valley. The corrie has a grassy floor with here and there gigantic boulders, the largest giving eight climbs from 15 to 25 feet. At places the stream is underground, and the exit from the corrie is through a perfect maze of boulders piled on top of each other, forming innumerable caves and underground passages. The stream here is quite out of sight but reappears on the steep descent to the Coe. At its junction with the Coe are some very fine pools, but there should be no difficulty in crossing the main stream.

An interesting route to Bidean is up the Allt Coire Gabhail to its head, and thence up steep scree slopes to the summit cairn.

There are one or two good rock climbs in this corrie, in particular the Lost Valley Buttress which stands at the head

E

and leads up to the middle of the ridge between Bidean and Stob Coire Sgreamhach.

Other routes to Bidean are from Coire nam Beith to the saddles west or east of Stob Coire nam Beith, and to the saddle immediately to the west of Bidean up the scree slopes beside the Church Door Buttress.

Bidean nam Bian can also be climbed from Dalness in Glen Etive by Gleann Fhaolain, but this route is more commonly used on the descent—sometimes in error.

Beinn Fhada (3120 feet).—As already explained above, Beinn Fhada can be climbed easily from Coire Gabhail. It can also be reached from the Lairig Eilde, the path which leads from Dalness in Glen Etive to the Study in Glencoe, passing to the west of Buachaille Etive Beag.

Stob Coire nan Lochan (3657 feet).—This is a very fine-looking mountain, well seen from the Study. With its sharp peak rising above the snow-clad N.E. corrie it is usually taken to be Bidean nam Bian itself. The usual line of ascent is from the ridge connecting it with Bidean, but it may be ascended anywhere from Coire nam Beith provided the climber does not object to 500 feet of screes of the most heart-breaking type. Other routes, more or less rock-climbs, lead up over its two outlying buttresses, Geàrr Aonach and Aonach Dubh, or up the stream between the two buttresses.

Geàrr Aonach (2500 feet) is the prominent rocky termination of the N.E. ridge of Stob Coire nan Lochan. It presents a very bold appearance to Glencoe with its almost perfect rock cone standing out as a separate peak. Beinn Fhada, Geàrr Aonach, and Aonach Dubh are the famous Three Sisters of Glencoe, and it is their rugged beauty, combined perhaps with the massacre, which has made this Glen the most famous and picturesque in Scotland. Geàrr Aonach can also be climbed from Coire Gabhail, but an easy rock-climb may be had right up the face. The rock is porphyry and excellent for climbing. This route was made by Naismith, Maclay, and Boyd at Easter 1898, and they descended by a parallel route some 30 or 40 yards farther east.

Aonach Dubh (2849 feet).—This fine buttress is perhaps the most imposing of the Three Sisters, its great rock bastion " beetling o'er its base " above the dark waters of Loch Achtriochtan. High up on its face is the Cave of Ossian, a black slit like a gigantic keyhole. Nicol Marquis, a Glencoe shepherd, is supposed to have made the first ascent into the cave about 1868. The last 100 feet up to the Cave is very steep rock, and to the left of the Cave is a buttress of fine porphyry which affords good rock-climbing. A fairly easy way up Aonach Dubh is to follow the right bank of the gorge, which comes down from the ledge below the Cave, until the ledge is reached. The ledge is then followed diagonally up to the right and well round the face of the mountain until the rocks cease and scree slopes lead to the summit.

Stob Coire nam Beith (3621 feet).—This is the bold rocky pyramid which is so well seen from the Glen near Clachaig Inn. The usual route is from Coire nam Beith (reached as described on p. 56) up to the saddle to the west of the peak. An interesting route involving a little scrambling can be made from the corrie directly up the N.W. slopes to the cairn. The rocks to the left of this route are very steep and afford some first-rate climbs.

An t-Sròn (2750 feet approx.)—This is the prominent grassy point south-east of Clachaig Inn with the very conspicuous gully splitting the north face almost from summit to base. The best route up is from Coire nam Beith or from the west. The north face is interrupted by rocky outcrops.

Rock Climbs

Excellent rock-climbing is to be had on almost all the peaks of this group. The principal climbs will be described in the order of their respective peak as given above.

BIDEAN NAM BIAN

The Church Door Buttress.—This well-known rock-climb is situated at the head of Coire nam Beith, right under the summit cairn of Bidean nam Bian. Looking up from Glencoe where the new road branches off from the old road near Clachaig Inn, the twin buttresses which form the actual summit of the mountain can just be seen. The right-hand buttress is the Church Door, while the left-hand, or more northerly, is now known as the Diamond Buttress. Owing to their being farther away, these buttresses are somewhat dwarfed by the imposing cone-shaped crags of Stob Coire nam Beith, which from here present an unusually fine mountain view.

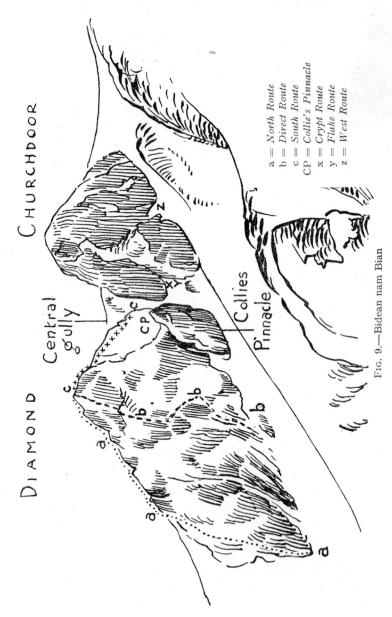

a = North Route
b = Direct Route
c = South Route
CP = Collie's Pinnacle
x = Crypt Route
y = Flake Route
z = West Route

FIG. 9.—Bidean nam Bian

BIDEAN NAM BIAN

The Diamond Buttress and the Church Door Buttress.

(see Fig. 9.)

The Church Door climb had resisted many strenuous onslaughts before it was at last conquered in July 1898 by Harold Raeburn, J. H. Bell, H. C. Boyd, and R. G. Napier. The former attempts by many well-known climbers such as Collie, Hastings, Collier, and Solly, in addition to the successful party, had all been made under bad conditions, and were foiled by weather or iced rocks. When at last good weather and summer conditions favoured the climbers, immediate success was theirs. Bell led triumphantly up to the arch, and Raeburn conquered the upper chimney. There has been no recorded ascent since, under genuine winter conditions.

In misty weather, if the climber can find his way up the glen past the cliffs of Stob Coire nam Beith, he should reach an upper shallow corrie with the lip composed of smooth slabs. On the right will be found a great mass of boulders and scree, and directly over this lies the way up to Collie's Pinnacle, which stands at the foot of the gully separating the twin buttresses.

The route lies up the gully, keeping the Pinnacle on the left. Just below the neck connecting the Pinnacle with the upper gully an enormous crack will be noticed on the right, splitting the buttress from top to bottom. An easy traverse across leads to the foot of the crack. This goes quite easily, and lands the climber on the crest of the buttress. The other side of the crack can also be climbed and is reached by traversing round the outside of the flake about 50 feet lower down the gully. The next move is rather a delicate step round a corner to the right, on to the main buttress. A short chimney and some easy rocks lead to a level traverse which runs to the left to the arch of the Church Door. The arch is formed by two enormous jammed boulders, through the gaps in which one can look down about 200 feet to the screes below. The second man belays on the arch, while the leader crosses two slabs which slope outwards from the base of the famous chimney which is the crux of the climb. The chimney is started facing to the right, and then a few feet up it is necessary to face in and endeavour to reach a hold below the small jammed block. A climber with a short reach will find some difficulty here, and it may be necessary to push up a bight of the rope over the hold, and so in this unorthodox way pull up until the right hand can reach the jammed block.   Above this, the route goes straight up over a steep little face before the easy ground leading to the cairn on Bidean nam Bian is reached.   If one goes left to avoid the face an obvious chimney is seen, but this is more difficult. The climb is about 350 feet.

The first variation on the original route, the Crypt Route, was made by Wood, Wilding and Pigott in September 1920. It starts a few yards to the left of the ordinary route and follows the line of a chimney to the right-hand end of the Arch.   About 70 feet up the chimney, a rock corridor is reached which leads more or less underground.   Here there is a choice of routes;   the Tunnel Route limited to those with a shoulder span of not more than 18 inches;   and the Through Route which provides a sensational and overhanging exit from a small cave.

In the first Edition of this Guide, it was suggested that a possible route might be found on the west face of the Buttress up to the Arch.   This important variation was made in July 1937 by W. H. Murray, J. K. W. Dunn and W. G. Marskell. The start is from the prominent bay seen in the photograph (p. 60) just to the right of the lower rocks of the Buttress. The route goes up to the left to the outer edge of the buttress above a bulge about 40 feet from the screes.   From here a shallow cleft springs vertically up towards the crest of the Buttress, and this is the key to the climb.   Above this a vertical wall of 15 feet leads to easier rocks and the original route below the Arch.

The Diamond Buttress.—The eastern or left-hand buttress of Bidean has not the picturesque appearance of its more famous neighbour.   At first sight it appears to be made up of grassy ledges and loose rock pitches of no interest to the climber.   Moreover, in addition to the Church Door Buttress, the very striking cliffs of Stob Coire nam Beith lie in wait for the climber on his way up from the glen, and their attractions would doubtless lure the impatient rock-climber from the unknown buttress at the head of the corrie.   Anyhow, it was not until 1930 that the buttress was properly explored. In August of that year J. H. B. Bell, Bartholomew, and A. Harrison made the first ascent of the buttress on its northern flank.   Not satisfied with this, Bell, returning in August 1931 with C. M. Allan, succeeded in making a difficult route up the centre line of the buttress, and by right of conquest christened it the Diamond Buttress. In addition to the two routes (a) and (b) shown on the accompanying diagram (Fig. 9), Bell also ascended the southern flank of the buttress by an easy route from above the neck of Collie's Pinnacle.

North Route (a).—This climb starts just north of the lowest point of the rocks and goes practically straight up, keeping a line well to the north of the summit. The lower rocks are steep but good, and not at all easy. About 60 feet up, the climber is forced a little to the left, and higher up it is possible in several cases to traverse to the north and so escape on to easy scree. The route, however, can be continued straight up over a succession of steep pitches separated by wide ledges. The climb finishes on a rock *arête* which runs southwards parallel to the main Stob Coire nan Lochan ridge and ends on the summit of the buttress. The climb is about 500 feet.

Direct Route (b).—The route starts from the screes directly in a line below the summit, and roughly half-way between the lowest rocks and Collie's Pinnacle. The climb goes diagonally to the right for 100 feet and then gradually back again to the centre line. The start is up broken rocks to a chimney behind a detached block and then to the right across the top of a chimney. The route now goes up to the left towards a pinnacle. Until a large moss-covered, overhanging block is reached, the angle is easier, but above the block, which offers no belay, there is a very steep and exposed section, leading to a steep little chimney above which is a good stance and belay. The pinnacle (P) is reached by a very difficult chimney on the left, and its summit is marked by a cairn. From here it would seem to be possible to traverse to the left on to the easier rocks of the North Route, but the ascent is continued directly up 100 feet of steep but easy rocks, then by a small pitch to behind a mammoth overhanging block, whence it is necessary to traverse to the right across a gap on to steep rocks with good holds. Again exits seemed to be possible both to right and left, but the direct route led up a difficult narrow chimney to a small recess from which an escape was made up a 10-foot wall on the right. There is one further short chimney difficulty, and the climb finishes within 80 feet of the cairn on the summit of the buttress. The height of the climb is about 500 feet ; generally speaking, the rock is sound and the belays are adequate. The first ascent was made in rubbers, and under perfect conditions took nearly four hours, so it must be considered " severe."

Collie's Pinnacle.—This pinnacle rises out of the lower part of the Central Gully, which runs up between the Church Door Buttress on the right and the Diamond Buttress on the left to the summit of Bidean. It was first explored and climbed by Professor Collie's party in 1894. On its lower side (west) overlooking the corrie, it is about 150 feet high, but on its upper side it only rises about 30 feet above the neck connecting it with the bed of the gully.

It can be climbed easily from this neck, although the last few feet are somewhat exposed, and also from the south branch of the gully just above the pitch. This latter route is longer, and although not difficult, the rocks are rather loose.

In May 1931 a route was made up from the north branch of the gully by J. H. B. Bell, G. R. Symmers, and W. B. Speirs, This climb starts low down in the gully, below the pitch. and leads up a 60-foot chimney to an oblong chock-stone. This was passed on the right wall with difficulty, and a good platform reached with a belay on a huge detached rock flake. Above this a short difficult wall was climbed, taking off from the flake. Then followed a short difficult chimney with a good belay at the foot. From here the summit of the pinnacle was reached over easy rocks.

In October 1931 the outside (west) face of the pinnacle was climbed by two climbers from Newcastle. The route lay up a crack which lies to the left of the south gully, and was very difficult.

Above the pitch in the north gully are two obvious cracks leading to the summit. The lower and longer one has probably been climbed.

STOB COIRE NAN LOCHAN

In the N.E. corrie of Stob Coire nan Lochan is a fine range of cliffs, consisting of a buttress directly under the peak, and three buttresses leading up to the ridge which runs out northwards to Aonach Dubh. Under winter conditions the beauty of this corrie is probably unmatched in the Central Highlands. Very few summer climbs have been

BIDEAN NAM BIAN

Looking up the north ridge with the Diamond Buttress on right.

THE CHURCH DOOR BUTTRESS
The start of the climb, showing the Crack and the Flake.

A. E. Robertson

GEÀRR AONACH, GLENCOE

The cliffs of Beinn Fhada appear on the left and of Stob Coire nan Lochan on the right skyline.

THE CLIFFS OF STOB COIRE NAN LOCHAN
(see Fig. 10)

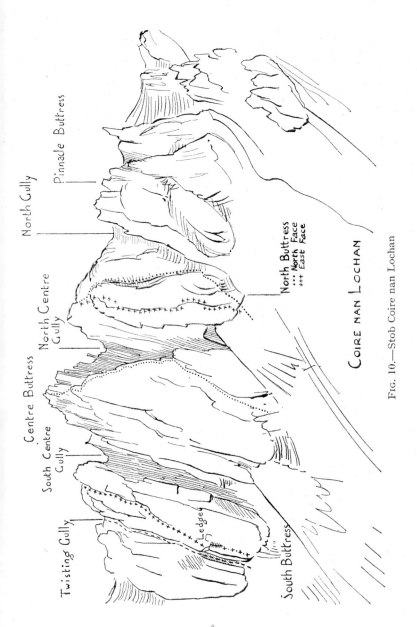

FIG. 10.—Stob Coire nan Lochan

done, however, as the rocks are very steep and slabby and not particularly well adapted for climbing, but excellent winter climbing is to be had of all grades of difficulty. They were first climbed in May 1894 by Collie, Solly, and Collier, but no description of their route is available.

Summit Buttress.—In September 1931 J. H. B. Bell and C. M. Allan climbed the rocks directly below the summit cairn, and christened their route the Summit Buttress. The lower part of the climb (350 feet) is the buttress proper. The buttress is joined by a col to the upper part of the mountain, which consists of steep broken-up rocks which afford good scrambling for about 350 feet right up to the summit cairn. Just to the right of the lowest rocks of the buttress will be seen an undercut chimney, with a curious hole in its roof about 40 feet up. The route goes up the wall to the right of the chimney by ledges to an open corner, and then by difficult balance movements to the right to a good anchorage ; then up diagonally to the left for 100 feet over very steep rock brings the climber to the crux of the climb. Here there is a convenient rocky corner with a block above a crack on the left. The key to the pitch is a hold behind and below the block. Then follow in succession a short traverse to the left, an overhanging wall, and a long inclined chimney leading obliquely up to the right. The climb finishes up a short steep crack to the col.

Central Buttress.—In April 1907 Harold Raeburn, Dr. and Mrs Inglis Clark, and C. Inglis Clark ascended the central of the three buttresses on the north ridge. This buttress projects the farthest into the corrie, and its lower portion is less steep. The route starts in a recessed corner on the left, where the upper cliff rises steeply above the lower section and goes straight up over steep rocks with good handholds to the crest of the ridge. From here easier rocks lead up the ridge to a prominent tower visible from below. The tower is circumvented on the left. The first step is round into a corner beyond which rises the tower. A possible route might be made up this corner and the chimney above it. The way, however, lies farther to the left by an awkward and exposed traverse, which leads to a short chimney above which one soon gains the main ridge of the mountain, directly above the tower.

North Buttress.—The north face was climbed by Bell and Allan in September 1931. The lower portion was not steep but gave about 150 feet of quite difficult climbing on loose rocks and turfy ledges. Between this portion and the upper cliffs of columnar basalt is a grassy hump. The upper cliffs are appallingly steep on the left, with an acute edge facing N.N.E. The only route was on the right or north face, by a series of loose ledges up about 200 feet to the crest of the cliff, where the final *arête* is nearly level. The upper part of this climb has not much to recommend it.

The east face which is " severe," was climbed by D. H. Haworth and Hughes in July 1947.

South Buttress.—This was climbed by the Ledge Route in November 1936 by Edo Derzaj and E. A. M. Wedderburn. It starts from the foot of Twisting Gully and goes up the left-hand side of the buttress. The Direct Route, which is more difficult, was climbed in September 1941. The routes join one-third of the way up.

The gully between the North and Central Buttresses seems to be easy throughout, but the gully between the South and Central Buttresses is steep, with most impressive rock scenery. The lower part has two pitches, 30 feet and 70 feet, and requires some care. Under winter conditions the gully, which is about 500 feet, gives one of the best climbs in the district. It was first climbed under these conditions by P. D. Baird, Leslie and Clinton in March 1934.

Twisting Gully (450 feet) is a deep groove on the left flank of South Buttress. It is a winter climb of " severe " standard and one of the best on Bidein. The first 100 feet twists up to a small crag dividing the gully—hence the name. It was climbed in December 1946 by W. H. Murray, D. Scott and J. C. Simpson.

To the north of the three buttresses there is a crazy-looking pinnacle, but the rocks here are so shattered that it is improbable that any climbing of note will be found in this quarter.

THE OSSIAN'S CAVE FACE OF AONACH DUBH

One of the most attractive crags for rock-climbing in the Glencoe region is undoubtedly the upper cliff of Aonach Dubh facing Loch Achtriochtan. The huge rift of Ossian's Cave

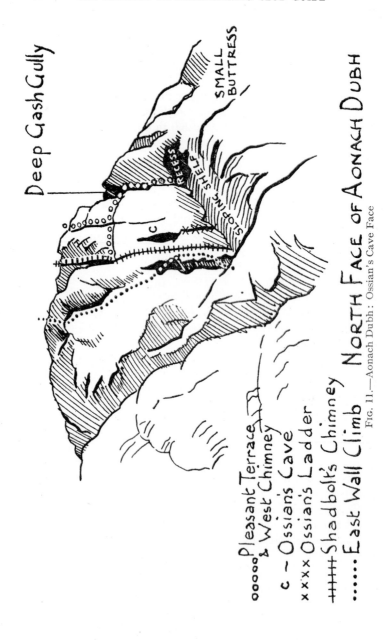

ooooo Pleasant Terrace & West Chimney
c – Ossians Cave
xxxx Ossian's Ladder
++++ Shadbolt's Chimney
...... East Wall Climb

NORTH FACE of AONACH DUBH

Fig. 11.—Aonach Dubh : Ossian's Cave Face

is the central feature of the crag, and the obvious line of approach is up the eastern ridge bounding the great waterfall gully which cleaves the lower front of Aonach Dubh. By continuing as far as possible up this ridge it is possible by an easy traverse on the right to attain the long inclined sloping shelf which passes upwards in a westerly direction past the foot of Shadbolt's Chimney and Ossian's Ladder. This Shelf leads straight up into the base of a tremendous unclimbed gully, Deep Gash Gully, and then continues past a fine 200-foot porphyry buttress, gradually ascending until a short, easy, deep-cut gully pierces the upper band of cliffs and gives access to the final slopes of Aonach Dubh. This is the easiest route up this face, involving no actual rock climbing.

To the right of the great waterfall gully, the mountain is crossed diagonally by shelves running up from left to right. The continuation of some of these shelves will be found crossing the precipitous western face of the mountain so well seen from Clachaig Inn. The highest shelf is the one referred to above as the easiest route to the summit. A fairly easy route can be made here, climbing from shelf to shelf and finishing by the easy deep-cut gully above the highest shelf, or on screes further west.

High up on the cliff above Ossian's Cave is the Pleasant Terrace. It is reached from the recess below Deep Gash Gully by a shallow trap gully, and leads horizontally across the face from Deep Gash Gully to the grassy amphitheatre above Shadbolt's Chimney. Near the middle of the Terrace is the deep slit of the West Chimney which gives an easy route to the top of the cliffs.

East Wall Climb.—From near the east end of the sloping Shelf starts apparently the route followed by Professor Collie, G. A. Solly, and J. Collier in March 1894, and by Wm. Brown and Tough in July 1895, but from the descriptions left it is not possible to identify exactly the routes followed. In an endeavour to locate these routes, J. H. B. Bell and Professor Turnbull, in December 1932, started from the shelf up a rock and grass recess in a westerly direction. The first section was distinctly awkward, with a difficult corner—a kind of turfy half-chimney. This section might be about 80 feet in height. A small group of ash trees clinging to the cliff face was left below on the right. An easier section

followed, still turfy. This was not very steep. Above, it
seemed to be possible to traverse to the left, past a sensational
corner, and on to easier ground. The only belay was not
well placed, however. They decided to take the direct route,
which was up a vertical chimney in two sections. The lower
section, about 25 feet in height, was interesting but of moderate
difficulty. The upper section of 30 feet was, however, very
difficult. It was necessary to trust entirely to an awkwardly
placed chock-stone at the most difficult part. Bell tested
this carefully and believes it to be sound. Above the difficult
section is a 10-foot exit on to the right wall. They were now
on relatively easy ground, about 350 feet above the shelf.
A step or two to their right was the shallow middle section
of Shadbolt's Chimney. An easy exit was clearly available
on the eastern or left side up a stepped and slabby staircase
of rock. The direct route, however, continues ahead. A
little to the left of Shadbolt's upper chimney is a very steep,
shallow chimney with a curious stairlike appearance. This
would lead to the upper exit from Shadbolt's Chimney. Still
farther to the left was the continuation of their route. First
came a long constricted, trap chimney, at least 60 feet in
height. A more constricted and difficult short section of
10-15 feet succeeded this. Then a long 80-100-foot section
led to a wide upper recess. From this 200-300 feet of broken
rocks led to the summit of Aonach Dubh.

Shadbolt's Chimney.—Farther west along the shelf and
only a few yards from the foot of Ossian's Ladder will be
found a deeply cut chimney. This is the start of a fine climb
made by A. C. M'Laren and L. G. Shadbolt in June 1908.
The chimney leads upwards for about 150 feet, after which
its character changes and its shallow continuation runs up
to the top of the buttress. The first deeply cut portion gives
fine climbing with back and knee. At the top of this, to
avoid loose rock, a short traverse was made out to the right
on to the buttress and then up 20 feet to a grassy ledge.
From here the leader stepped back to the left into the chimney
again and tackled a very steep pitch of 80 feet, where the
holds were just sufficient. The next difficulty was a 30-foot
chimney overhanging at the top. A large spike of rock in
the bed of the chimney served as a belay for Shadbolt, who,
standing in a niche just under the overhang, safeguarded the
leader over the next few feet.

Beyond this upper pitch the climbing is fairly easy for a short distance, until a spacious grassy amphitheatre is entered. The natural exit to the top of the cliff is straight ahead, up a wide trap gully called *The Corridor*, which rises to a great notch in the skyline. This gully is abominably loose at some parts, and the ascending climbers must keep close together. It is also difficult, and very steep. The height of this final section is at least 150 feet, probably more. The Corridor may be avoided on the outside right wall. The exit leads out on to easy broken rocks near the summit of Aonach Dubh.

Ossian's Cave.—The next climb to the right is Ossian's Cave itself. The way lies up the misnamed Ossian's Ladder, which leads up from the shelf, the route to which has already been mentioned. The Ladder used to be about 100 feet of most objectionable disintegrated vegetation and rock ; it is now swept clean and the rock has good holds and belays. In the so-called cave the vegetation is luxurious and the floor at an angle of 45 degrees ! A metal box containing the names of visitors will be found at the back of the cave. In August 1930 the box was opened and found to contain 49 names, starting in 1897 with the time-honoured name of W. Cecil Slingsby. A new box containing all the names now replaces the old one.

CLIMBS ON THE EAST FACE OF AONACH DUBH

This East Face is a range of rhyolite cliffs about 600 feet high which extends some 400 yards along the valley leading up into Coire nan Lochan. It was first explored in 1947. The rock is sound, clean and rough, and 9 routes have been made up it varying from " difficult " to " severe."

CLIMBS ON THE WEST FACE OF AONACH DUBH

This face of Aonach Dubh is held to cover all the buttresses and gullies which face Clachaig, irrespective of whether they are on Aonach Dubh proper or on the north-west ridge of Stob Coire nan Lochan, the northern termination of which is Aonach Dubh. The face is divided vertically by six gullies, and horizontally by a ledge and a rake, forming three tiers of rock. The rake is under the final tier and is broad and well broken up. The ledge under the middle tier is narrow. The photo facing p. 72 and Fig. 12 show the various rock buttresses with their dividing gullies very clearly. The

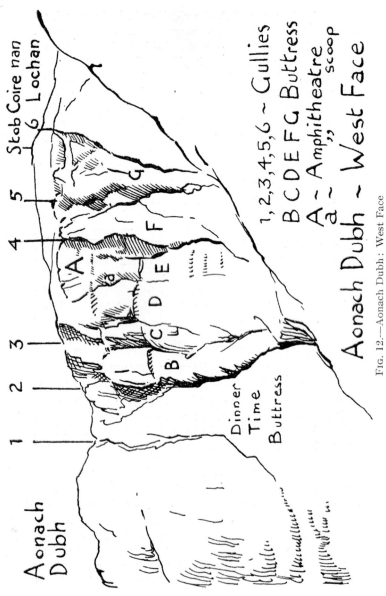

FIG. 12.—Aonach Dubh: West Face

THE WEST CLIFFS OF AONACH DUBH

(see Fig. 12)

STOB COIRE NAM 'BEITH
(see Fig. 13)

L. St. C. Bartholomew

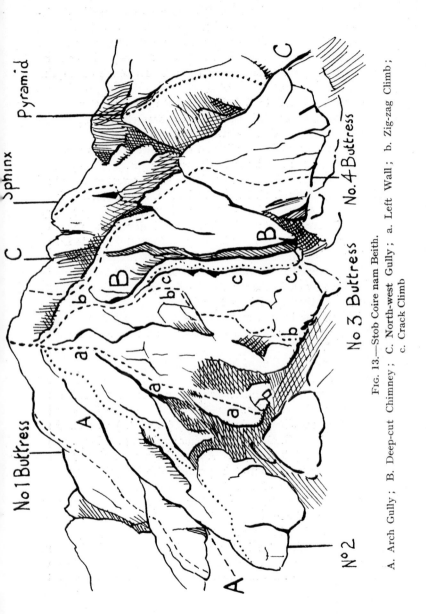

Fig. 13.—Stob Coire nam Beith.

A. Arch Gully ; B. Deep-cut Chimney ; C. North-west Gully ; a. Left Wall ; b. Zig-zag Climb ; c. Crack Climb

most prominent gully (No. 2) runs up to the col between Aonach Dubh and Stob Coire nan Lochan, and is a fairly easily identifiable landmark even in the worst weather.

On the left or north of No. 2 gully is the easy Dinner Time Buttress, and on its left is No. 1 gully.   These are both quite easy.

Gullies Nos. 2 to 6 have not been climbed throughout under summer conditions, but No. 3 was climbed in March 1934 after 6 hours' step-cutting by Crofton and Evans.

No. 2 gully has been climbed in its lower part as a means of access to the fine buttress (B) on its right.

B. Buttress.—The upper portion of (B) buttress was climbed in May 1932 by J. H. B. Bell and C. M. Allan, starting from the ledge above the lowest tier of cliffs.   This porphyry buttress gives an interesting but easy climb on good rock.

The Direct Route up this Buttress from the Middle Ledge was made by A. S. Parker and H. G. Nicol in June 1948, and is " hard severe."   A route by the North Wall was made in July 1946 by N. Tennant and Miss McLeod and is only a little less severe than the Direct Route.

This is the biggest and finest of the seven buttresses and the Direct Route on it is the hardest on this West Face of Aonach Dubh.

The upper portion of No. 3 gully was climbed by Mr and Mrs G. D. Abraham in October 1900, starting also from the same ledge as Bell and Allan.   They reached the ledge by the lower portion of No. 2 gully.

The scoop between buttresses (D) and (E) was climbed by Mr and Mrs G. D. Abraham after exploring the lower parts of buttresses (C) and (D).   Above the second tier of cliffs this scoop opens out into the amphitheatre (A), which extends south to the top of No. 4 gully.   In the amphitheatre is Winifred's Pinnacle, named after Mrs Abraham, and also another fine pinnacle explored and climbed by J. H. B. Bell and C. M. Allan in May 1932.

The Amphitheatre is the large high-level basin between the upper tiers of D. and F. Buttresses.   It is a corrie well worth visiting, as the rock scenery is spectacular and probably unique in the Central Highlands.

Apart from the Pinnacles referred to, the Central Ridge provides a very fine although " severe " climb of 200 feet.

The lower part is a sharp *arête*. The upper part is a buttress. It was climbed in November 1935 by J. H. B. Bell and C. M. Allan.

At Easter 1898 J. Maclay, Dr. Inglis Clark, and J. Gall Inglis made a route up the lowest tier of buttress (*E*). The second tier was climbed in No. 4 gully and then a traverse along and down the ledge below the third tier took them into No. 5 gully. The third tier of rock was climbed by " a steep knife-edge *arête* " in the centre of this gully.

C. Buttress.—The climb is on one tier only between Middle Ledge and the Rake.

D. Buttress is squat, broad and undercut. It is not difficult.

E. Buttress is unclimbed.

F. Buttress.—This is an interesting climb of 450 feet. It starts from the base of the waterfall from No. 5 gully.

G. Buttress is small and nondescript. There is no record of any climb here.

No. 6 gully does not appear to be climbable, as there are two long water-slide pitches, apparently quite holdless.

Stob Coire nam Beith

The north face of Stob Coire nam Beith gives very interesting climbing under both summer and winter conditions. From the new bridge over the Coe near Clachaig Inn a fine view is obtained of the Stob with its symmetrical cone of dark rock towering above the gorge of the Allt Coire nam Beith, and quite dwarfing the Church Door Buttress of Bidean which appears to the left. Following the usual route up the stream to where it forks at about 1500 feet, the climber turns left, and keeping to the left bank of the main branch reaches the remains of the old deer fence about 2000 feet. Bearing to the right, in about 150 yards, the foot of a scree slope is reached. This slope has come down fan-shaped, and its apex shown on Fig. 13 at B is a convenient key for the climbs on the face. To the right of the scree the cliffs gradually swing round to the west and south-west, and become more broken up. On the left are the finest rocks and gullies, with two large patches of green moss as notable landmarks, and then as the corrie rises and the cliffs gradually swing round to the south-east easier ground with open gullies and smaller rock-faces.

Starting from the east there is first a broken-up ridge running down from near the col to the east of the top. To the west of this ridge the cliffs are slightly set-back to form No. 1 Buttress, bounded on the east by a broken-up, easy gully and on the west by a rather imposing looking gully which appears to run from the actual peak right down to the corrie. This gully is the Arch Gully.

No. 1 Buttress between the two gullies is in two tiers, separated by a large, more or less level platform. The lower tier is cut from top to bottom by a chimney, which also appears again in the upper tier. The buttress was climbed in 1928 by A. Harrison, N. Allan, and A. J. Don. Starting to the left of the chimney, after 20 feet an upward traverse across the chimney for some 50 feet was made. Thereafter the line of the chimney was roughly followed on the right side. The last 100 feet are steeper and the rock is not good. The climb is about 700 feet.

The Arch Gully to the right of No. 1 Buttress was first climbed in its lower parts by Mr and Mrs G. D. Abraham in 1900. The first pitch is short and wet, and can be avoided on the left wall. After several small pitches comes the arch, formed by a huge elliptical chock-boulder, followed by a pitch which is climbed on the right wall. Thereafter the long middle section is a walk. The upper section is steep and narrow, running up over three well-defined, difficult chimney pitches for about 120 feet to a lip. The first party climbed this section on the left wall. Above the lip the angle eases off and the gully opens out into a little corrie about 400 feet from the summit cairn.

No. 2 Buttress is to the west of the Arch Gully, and is distinguished by the two very large patches of green moss on its western side. A route has been made up its left side, starting at a height of about 2500 feet and following at first the line of a shallow chimney. The top of the buttress is about 3100 feet.

No. 3 Buttress is separated from No. 2 by the green patches and some indefinite grass gullies and rakes. It is the finest of the cliffs in the Bidean group and rises from the corrie to the summit cairn in a succession of rocky steps about 1300 feet in all. The scree slope already referred to comes down from the gullies and chimney which form the western boundary of the buttress. The buttress can be climbed by a zigzag route, starting up to the right or west of the green patches, and going thereafter straight up the upper tiers of rock to the summit.

A good route has been made to the left of this Centre Route or zig-zag route called Left Wall. It keeps well to the left of the green moss patches but later trends to the right. After the first 400 feet the route is indefinite but continues up another 600 feet of easy rocks.

The Crack Climb was the earliest serious climb to be tackled on this face. It follows the line of the prominent crack which runs up the buttress to the left of the very prominent deep-cut gully between Nos. 3 and 4 Buttresses. It is reached from the top of the scree slope. After several winter attempts it was finally climbed in July 1912 by J. H. Hirst and R. E. Workman. This is one of the best climbs on Stob Coire nam Beith. It has not been climbed under real winter conditions.

It starts up 80 feet of steep rock to the foot of the crack, where there is good anchorage. Then 70 feet up the crack to a recess ; 80 feet of easier climbing leads to a grass platform. A little above the platform the rocks to the right of the crack are climbed, as the crack itself has become very narrow and overhanging a deep undercut forming a small cave. Above this a traverse is made on a broad, grassy ledge for about 50 feet towards the gully on the right, and then up a vertical wall with small holds. Still keeping to the right of the crack, another 100 feet leads to the top of the steep part.

Deep-cut Chimney. This is the narrow chimney between No. 3 and No. 4 Buttress. It starts at the head of the fan-shaped scree slope already referred to. The gully ends in a small amphitheatre about 400 feet up, but the climb continues 100 feet by a left or right fork to join either No. 3 or No. 4 Buttress routes. This gully gives an excellent winter climb.

No. 4 Buttress.—This buttress lies between Deep-cut Chimney and North-West Gully.

The large open gully slanting up to the right from Deep-cut Chimney is quite easy, and numerous routes can be made, starting up this gully and following up the easy rocks and grassy rakes on the north-western slopes of the Stob. Many of the separate rock pitches are difficult, but there does not appear to be any continuous rock-climb, and the face is more suitable for climbing when under snow and ice.

North-West Gully lies to the right of No. 4 Buttress and runs up the north-west face some 900 feet from right to left towards the actual summit. It was climbed in September 1931 by Ian Campbell and Horne. There are two pitches near the foot which have not yet been climbed direct but are avoided by rocks on the right. The first winter ascent was made in April 1906 by G. T. Glover and R. W. Worsdell. About 250 feet below the summit the gully forks. The left branch is the better and contains a good 12-foot pitch and an amusing chimney with so many jammed blocks as to convert it into a tunnel.

The two prominent buttresses which appear in the photograph above North-West Gully have both been climbed. The upper one, slightly to the left, is the Sphinx (450 feet) and is the steepest cliff on the mountain. The lower and right-hand one is the Pyramid (300 feet).

AN T-SRÒN

North Gully.—This prominent gully, which splits the north face, was explored and climbed by J. H. B. Bell and J. M'Nab at Easter 1932. It starts about the 1000-foot contour and finishes about 2250 feet, but the greater part of it is just a walk.

The first pitch is a great waterfall which overhangs. This is avoided by climbing out of the gully on the right (100 feet), and then traversing back in again among birch trees. The second pitch (20 feet) is climbed on the right wall, with a step across to the chock-stone at the top. There follows a long easy stretch (100 yards), with an exit on the left (east). The gully then forks, the left branch petering out, and the right branch leading to the third pitch, another waterfall. This is difficult, with the best holds in the waterfall. A little higher is yet another waterfall pitch, much easier, and above this fourth pitch there is about 600 feet with no climbing. This leads to the fifth and last pitch, about 20 feet of black slimy rock and moss. The route goes up the right wall, and then a straddle across to the left wall gets the climber up reasonably dry. Above this the gully gradually merges into the face of the hill, which is here steep and broken up by numerous outcrops of rock.

IX

BEINN A' BHEITHIR
(The Peak of the Thunder-bolt.)

THIS beautiful mountain group is situated on the south side of Loch Leven, near its junction with Loch Linnhe. The principal tops are as follows :—

(1) **Sgòrr Dhearg** (3362 feet) = the red peak. 2½ miles S. of Ballachulish Ferry.

(2) **Sgòrr Dhonuill** (3284 feet) = Donald's Peak. 1 mile W. by S. of (1).

(3) Creag Ghorm (2372 feet) = the blue rock. 2 miles N.W. of (1).

(4) Sgòrr a' Chaolais (2700 feet) = peak of the narrows. ½ mile N.E. of (2).

(5) Sgòrr Bhan (3104 feet) = the white peak. ⅓ mile E.N.E. of (1).

All the summits with the exception of No. 4 lie on the main ridge, which forms a great horseshoe circling round from Creag Ghorm above Ballachulish Pier, 1 mile west of the Ferry to Sgòrr Bhan and its outlying nose Beinn Bhan (1645 feet) above Ballachulish village.

The usual route is by Gleann a' Chaolais up to the main ridge about 2700 feet, just west of Sgòrr Dhonuill, which is here a broad plateau with numerous little tops with marshy ground or in some cases little lochans in between. A gentle rise of about 500 feet leads to the sharp top of Sgòrr Dhonuill (3284 feet). A fairly steep drop of 800 feet leads to the bealach between the twin peaks, and from here an easy way will be found back into Gleann a' Chaolais, and so home. From the bealach a well-defined ridge runs up to the culminating summit of the group Sgòrr Dhearg (3362 feet).

The views from the tops of Ben Vare (as it is pronounced) are specially fine, extending as they do from the open sea over the picturesque mountains of Morven and Ardgour to the Mamores and Ben Nevis. To the east there is Loch Leven and the magnificent Glencoe mountains.

From Sgòrr Dhearg a pleasant route for the descent is down the narrow north ridge which takes one almost straight back to the hotel at the Ferry.

The best excursion of all, however, is to start at the east

end and climb the west slopes of Beinn Bhan from the Allt Giùbhsachain. A narrow but very regular ridge leads up to Sgòrr Bhan (3104 feet) with steep corries on both sides. Thereafter it is a delightful high level walk right round to Creag Ghorm (2372 feet) with the most wonderful views out to the west. From Creag Ghorm a steep descent through the birch woods leads down to the road near Ballachulish Pier.

Sgòrr a' Chaolais (2700 feet approx.) is the sharp little horn so conspicuous just below and to the left of Sgòrr Dhonuill when viewed from North Ballachulish or even from Gleann a' Chaolais.

There is no rock-climbing on these mountains, but the late Colin B. Philip states that a good rock-scramble can be had up the gorge of the burn which rises on the plateau about $\frac{3}{4}$ mile west of Sgòrr Dhonuill and flows south-west into the River Duror.

The north-east ridge of Sgòrr Bhan is short and steep. It joins the north ridge referred to above, about $\frac{1}{4}$ mile north of the summit. It is of slaty rock, which forms ledges dipping across the ridge from north to south. Near the top the ridge is quite narrow, with one steep pitch which can be turned by ledges on the south. The ridge which runs south from Sgòrr Bhan appears also to be rocky and narrow, and might be worthy of exploration.

Dr. W. Inglis Clark

SGÒRR DHONUILL FROM NORTH ¦BALLACHULISH

April 1912

J. Rennie

LOOKING SOUTH FROM BIDEAN NAM BIAN

On left Glas Bheinn Mhòr, with Beinn nan Aighean and Beinn Eunaich appearing over ridge to Ben Starav ; Ben Cruachan (in mist) Loch Etive, and Beinn Trilleachan on right.

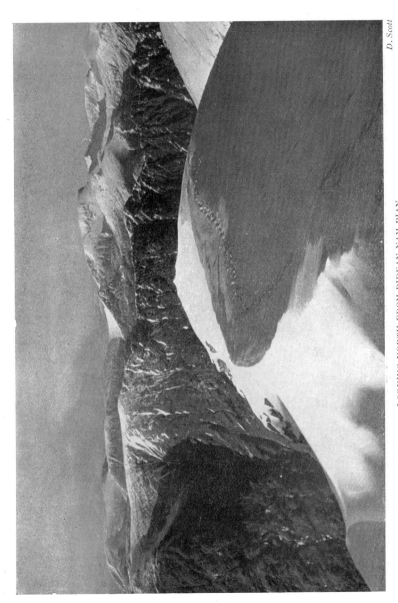

D. Scott

LOOKING NORTH FROM BIDEAN NAM BIAN

Aonach Eagach is in the middle distance. Behind Mullach nan Coirean, Stob Bàn, Ben Nevis and Càrn Mòr Dearg with Sgùrr a' Mhaim below. Aonach Mòr and Aonach Beag on extreme right.

A. E. Wormell

AONACH EAGACH

X

AONACH EAGACH

The Aonach Eagach, or Notched Ridge, is the name applied to the ridge which stretches along the north side of Glencoe for some 6 miles from the Pap of Glencoe to the Devil's Staircase. The following are the principal summits :—

(1) **Sgòr nam Fiannaidh** (3168 feet) = the peak of the Fianns. 1¼ miles N.N.E. of Clachaig Inn, Glencoe.

(2) Sgòr na Ciche (2430 feet) = Pap of Glencoe. 1¼ miles N.W. of (1).

(3) Stob Coire Lèith (3080 feet) = the peak of the grey corrie. ½ mile E. by N. of (1).

(4) **Meall Dearg** (3118 feet) = round red hill. ¾ mile E. of (3).

(5) Am Bodach (3085 feet) = the old man. ½ mile E.S.E. of (4).

(6) Sròn Garbh (2857 feet) = the rough nose. ¾ mile N. E. of (5).

(7) A'Chailleach (2938 feet) = the old woman. ¾ mile S.E. of (6).

(8) Garbh Bheinn (2835 feet) = the rough mountain. 1¼ miles N. by E. of (4).

The Aonach Eagach proper lies between Am Bodach in the east and Stob Coire Lèith in the west. This part of the ridge is the finest from the climber's point of view, and it is certainly the narrowest and most difficult of all the ridges on the mainland. The only ridges to compete with it are A'Chir in Arran, and, of course, several parts of the Cuillin ridge in Skye. In addition to the charm of the rugged and picturesque pinnacles on the ridge, the climber has most wonderful views of Bidean nam Bian on the south and of the Lochaber mountains and the deep valley of Loch Leven on the north.

The ridge is usually traversed from east to west, starting from the Glencoe road at the Study (900 feet) and going over Am Bodach to Sgòr nam Fiannaidh and then down to Clachaig Inn.

Another route is from Clachaig Inn to the Tartan Inn at Kinlochleven, over the ridge as far as Meall Dearg, and then due north to Garbh Bheinn and down the easterly ridge to the aluminium village ; or, again, the whole ridge can be traversed to Sròn Garbh, and down the Allt Coire Mhorair, joining the Devil's Staircase at a height of 500 feet and so down to Kinlochleven.

Sgòr nam Fiannaidh (3168 feet) is rather a featureless hill with regular scree slopes which should be avoided as much as possible in ascending. A good route is from the Glencoe road just east of where it crosses to the left bank of the Coe, $\frac{1}{4}$ mile above Clachaig Inn. Here will be found considerable grass slopes leading to the summit ridge to the east of the top.

Although a rather featureless hill taken as a whole, Sgòr nam Fiannaidh is the proud possessor of one of the finest gully climbs in all Scotland.

The Clachaig Gully.—This lies right above the Inn on the south slopes of the mountain. It starts about the 500-foot level and runs up to about the 2300-foot contour.

From below it does not appear as an attractive rock climb, looking more like an ordinary steep glen rather densely wooded. Up to about the 1000-foot level a perfect forest of birch and rowan trees sprout from the high walls amidst a profusion of wild flowers, shrubs and ferns, but as the walls approach the bed of the stream they draw closer together and the bare rock is exposed. Higher up, however, the walls become barer, the gully narrows and at one point becomes a mere chimney.

The first exploration was made in March 1894 by Norman Colie, Solly and Collier up to the foot of the Great Cave at about 1000 feet. In October 1900 an attempt was made by G. D. Abraham. W. B. Speirs reached the foot of the Great Cave in September 1931 and escaped on the left wall, and in September 1937 J. B. Nimlin climbed the Great Cave and escaped by a difficult route on the right wall.

The whole gully was eventually climbed in May 1938 by W. H. Murray, A. M. MacAlpine, J. K. W. Dunn and W. G. Marskell after three weeks of fine weather.

There are 30 pitches, of which 4 are " severe "—Great Cave, Jericho Wall, Red Chimney and Last Pitch.

There is no pitch so fierce of aspect as the Devil's Cauldron in the Chasm, but the general standard of difficulty is greater than in the Chasm, and it is some 300 feet longer. Five or six hours is now an adequate time-allowance for the climb.

From Sgòr nam Fiannaidh it is an easy walk over **Stob**

Coire Lèith (3080 feet) to the col beyond. This hill is called Meall Garbh on the one-inch map. From the col to **Meall Dearg** (3118 feet) is the best part of the ridge. Nowhere is it difficult, but it all requires care. A rope should be used not only to guard against the danger of a rotten hold giving way, but to give the climbers practice in handling a rope while moving fast over easy rocks. There is one specially good bit where a steep descent leads to a col with three crazy-looking pinnacles. These should be tackled direct, although it is possible to avoid them by a traverse lower down on the south side. The traverse of the ridge under real winter conditions is a splendid expedition.

The approach to Meall Dearg is very impressive, but it proves much easier than it looks. From here to Am Bodach is much simpler, although the ridge is still narrow, with precipitous drops on both sides.

Am Bodach (3085 feet) is not named on the one-inch map, but it is indicated by the 3000-foot contour. To reach the Study from here one must contour round the head of Coire an Ruigh, out of which flows the burn which comes down to the shepherd's cottage below the Study; or, of course, one can go right round the ridge over **Sròn Garbh** (2857 feet) to the Study, or even continue east over **A'Chailleach** (2938 feet) to the Devil's Staircase. This latter top is not named on the maps, but the name "A'Chailleach" appears on the one-inch map on the ridge running out from it towards the Study. The Devil's Staircase is the remains of the old military road from Altnafeadh (3 miles from Kingshouse) over to Kinlochleven.

One or two climbing routes have been made up the buttresses leading up to Aonach Eagach from Glencoe, but none of these is satisfactory or worth repeating. The rock is very rotten, especially lower down, and although it improves near the crest of the ridge it is always dangerous. The cliffs on the north side are much lower and quite as unsatisfactory. The large scree-filled gully which comes down from the east of Meall Dearg towards the shepherd's cottage at Achtriochtan can be descended easily, and also one coming down from the col east of Stob Coire Lèith. The two pitches near the foot can easily be avoided on the right. The south-west buttress of Am Bodach, to the right of the large gully referred to above, has also been climbed. Other easy routes can be worked out if one wishes to escape from the ridge, but, generally speaking, it is quicker to complete the ridge and descend from either the east or west end.

Sgòr na Ciche, or the Pap of Glencoe (2430 feet), is the very shapely cone-shaped mountain which separates lower Glencoe from Loch Leven. It is very steep on all sides, but there is no actual climbing on it. It is usually ascended from the neck connecting it with Sgòr nam Fiannaidh on the south-east.

Garbh Bheinn (2835 feet) is a fine sharp-pointed peak above Loch Leven, very conspicuous from the west and from the east, *e.g.*, from the railway near Rannoch Station. Apparently it was in the fastnesses of this mountain that Alan Breck Stewart and David Balfour, in *Kidnapped*, lay hidden after their escape in Glencoe and before they set out on their adventurous journey to the South.

XI

GLENCOE AND THE MOOR OF RANNOCH

GLENCOE is probably the most widely known and celebrated of all the Scottish glens. Not only is it famous historically for the dastardly massacre in 1692, but in more modern times, since the days of the tourist coaches, its wild austerity and gloomy impending crags have made it a popular show-place among all classes of travellers.

The River Coe rises on the southern slopes of Stob Mhic Mhartuin near the Devil's Staircase, and flows westwards through the famous glen for about 9 miles to the sea at Loch Leven.

The greater part of the glen itself is bare and without beauty ; a level trough, grassy, with neither heather, gorse, nor pine, around the little dark lochan at Achtriochtan. In this respect it cannot be compared with Glen Strathfarrar or Glen Affric. But viewed as a whole, and especially from its head near the Study, it presents an almost perfect picture of wild mountain grandeur. No other glen in Scotland, not even Glen Sligachan, can rival it in close-set rocky peak and deep-cut ravine. On both sides precipitous cliffs rise up from the green valley to over 3000 feet, and so apparently overhang their bases that one is not surprised to read early descriptions of the glen in which the travellers were in fear of being overwhelmed by the tottering masses. Looking down the glen the three great buttresses of Bidean nam Bian —Beinn Fhada, Geàrr Aonach, and Aonach Dubh—sometimes known as the Three Sisters of Glencoe, thrust their dark rocks out into the glen, ridge beyond ridge, with their abrupt lines soaring skyward and leading the eye to the graceful peak of Stob Coire nan Lochan. In contrast to the picturesque buttresses on the south side, the north of the glen is shut in by the great wall of the Aonach Eagach, the most broken-up and shattered ridge on the mainland. Here we have a whole array of black rock pinnacles cut off from each other by steep stone-swept gullies, one after the other in succession to the sentinel at the foot of the Glen, Sgòr nam Fiannaidh.

Unlike most other glens in Scotland, Glencoe shows up to greatest advantage when viewed from its head. Looking upstream the great bluff of Aonach Dubh cuts off most of the picturesque features on the right, while at the head of the glen there is no outstanding mountain form to fill in the gap.

In its lower reaches below Clachaig Inn the glen again completely changes its character. For 3 miles from Clachaig to Bridge of Coe the stream flows gently through a lowland valley with pasture lands and beautifully wooded slopes.

It was, no doubt, in this part of the glen that the greater part of the population lived at the time of the massacre, and here is to be found the monument to the memory of the fallen Macdonalds.

It will be recalled that after the Killiecrankie campaign the rebellious Highland chieftains were ordered to take the Oath of Allegiance to William III before 1st January 1692. The old chief of the Macdonalds, McIan of Glencoe, for various good reasons, was several days late, and this gave their heriditary foes, the Campbells, an opportunity for a complete and final revenge. Having many powerful friends at Court, they so contrived that orders were sent to Campbell of Glenlyon " to fall upon the Macdonalds of Glencoe and put all to the sword under 70." Accordingly, early in February 1692, a party of soldiers commanded by Glenlyon arrived in the glen and were billeted in the cottages. On the morning of the 13th the soldiers turned on their hosts and ruthlessly shot them down. Owing to bad staff-work the soldiers detailed to block the exits from the glen were late in taking up position, and many of the fugitives escaped, only, however, in some cases to perish in the snow. No effective steps were taken to punish the ringleaders in this ghastly plot.

In Stevenson's *Kidnapped* will be found a graphic description of the adventures of David Balfour and Alan Breck Stewart in Glencoe. It tells of their desperate leaps across the turbulent Coe, their refuge on the summit of two gigantic boulders, and their final flight among the numerous smaller boulders and heather to comparative safety above Kinloch-leven. Unfortunately, probably no highland glen has so few boulders, and certainly none has less heather !

The traveller going north to Glencoe by road or to Fort William by rail cannot fail to be impressed by the great desolate sweep of the Moor of Rannoch, or " Rannoch Muir " as it is designated on the one-inch Ordnance Survey. Here we have a more or less level wilderness of barren moor instead of the usual high mountain and deep glen. So level is it in parts that one could walk in a straight line for 10 miles between the 950- and 1000-foot contours.

The lowest elevation is in the south at Loch Tulla (540 feet), and it rises in various places to over 1600 feet, the highest point being 1795 feet.

In shape it is a gigantic triangle with its points roughly on Loch Tulla, Kingshouse Inn, and Loch Rannoch. Its western boundary (9 miles) is the Blackmount and the old Glencoe road ; its northern boundary (12 miles) is Stob na Gruaiche (2420 feet) and the high ground south of the Blackwater Reservoir ; its south-eastern boundary (14 miles) is the Beinn Dòrain group and the lower hills running N.E. to Loch Rannoch. The area is, therefore, about 56 square miles.

It sends its waters to Loch Etive and the Atlantic by way of the River Etive in the N.W. and the River Orchy in the S.W. The main drainage, however, goes to the North Sea by the River Bà, Loch Rannoch, the Tummel, and the Tay. The River Bà rises in Corrie Bà in the Blackmount and flows sluggishly through Lochan na Stainge, Loch Bà, and Loch Laidon, and thence to Loch Rannoch as the River Gaur. At Bà Bridge the level of the stream is 1046 feet, while at the railway bridge over the Gaur, 13 miles downstream, the level is 900 feet. Contrary to the general understanding, the Conan or River Coe does not rise on the Moor of Rannoch.

What was formerly the West Highland Railway to Fort William runs along the south-eastern margin of the Moor to Gorton Crossing and then turns more north and crosses very boggy ground to Rannoch Station. The permanent way is carried across this portion on floating brushwood. About 3½ miles south of Rannoch Station, beside the railway, are several lines of earth-works known as the " Soldiers' Trenches." These are the remains of a land reclamation scheme on the part of Ensign James Small, the " Gov. Factor to the then Forfeited Estate of Struan Robertson in 1763-65." [1] Ensign

---

[1] Vide *Forfeited Estate Papers* (Scottish History Society), p. 236.

Small, assisted by military labour, caused to be dug a series of five trenches to drain and sweeten the soil. Nothing came of the venture. There is also an old road and track from Bridge of Orchy past Achallader Farm and Castle to Gorton. This track formerly extended to the Soldiers' Trenches and continued N.E. to Loch Rannoch by the path down Gleann Chomraidh.

The new Glencoe road leaves the old road at Bridge of Orchy and, running round the head of Loch Tulla, passes between Lochan na Stainge and Loch Bà and cuts across the old road just south of Kingshouse Inn. The old road skirts the Moor on the west side, keeping generally to the higher ground, and rises to 1454 feet at the Bà Pass. A short track runs from this road near Bà Cottage east to Loch Bà. The old road is closed to motor traffic.

The only other track across the Moor runs from Rannoch Station westwards to Kingshouse Inn, about 13 miles. At first the path skirts the shores of Loch Laidon and is fairly good, but when it turns west near Tigh na Cruaiche and contours across the higher ground about the 1150-foot level it practically disappears. At the Black Corries Lodge, however, a driving road is reached, and 4 miles along this brings one to Kingshouse Inn.

The situation of the Moor, with its encircling and picturesque peaks, makes it quite unique from the scenic point of view, although somewhat similar effects on a smaller scale may be obtained in Sutherlandshire. One cannot do better than quote here from Principal Shairp's well-known poem on the Moor :

> Beuchaille Etive's furrowed visage
>   To Schihallion looked sublime,
> O'er a wide and wasted desert
>   Old and unreclaimed as time.
>
> Yea ! a desert wide and wasted,
>   Washed by rainfloods to the bones,
> League on league of heather blasted,
>   Storm-gashed moss, grey boulder-stones.
>
> Mountain girdled—there Bendoran
>   To Schihallion calls aloud,
> Beckons he to lone Ben-Aulder,
>   He to Nevis crowned with cloud.

AN GARBHANACH
From the South.

N. L. Hird

AONACH BEAG

With N.E. Ridge showing just to right of the summit, and Ben Nevis appearing
over the col to Aonach Mòr.

As a counterblast to the above, the Rev. John Lettice, " Poet and Divine," sometime rector of Peasmarch, in Sussex, and later chaplain to the Duke of Hamilton, in his *Letters on a Tour through various Parts of Scotland in the year* 1792," writes of the Moor :

> " An immense vacuity, with nothing in it to contemplate, unless numberless mis-shapen blocks of stone rising hideously above the surface of the earth, would be said to contradict the inanity of our prospects."

G

XII

THE MAMORES

THIS large group of fine mountains lies between Glen Nevis on the north and Loch Leven on the south. The main ridge or backbone runs east and west for about 7 miles, throwing out three important ridges to the north. Although the name Mamore would seem to indicate gently swelling hills, the peaks are mostly bold and picturesque and the ridges narrow and well defined. The principal summits are as follows :—

(1) **Mullach nan Coirean** (3077 feet)=the rounded hill of the corries. 5 miles S.S.E. of Fort William.

(2) Mullach nan Coirean, S.E. top (3004 feet). ¾ mile S.E. of (1).

(3) **Stob Bàn** (3274 feet)=the white mountain. 1 mile E. of (2).

(4) **Sgùrr a' Mhaim** (3601 feet)=the crag of the pass. 1¼ miles N.E. of (3).

(5) Sgòr an Iubhair (3300 feet)=the peak of the yew tree. ¾ mile S. of (4).

(6) **Am Bodach** (3382 feet)=the old man. ¾ mile E.S.E. of (5).

(7) **Stob Coire a' Chairn** (3219 feet)=peak of the corrie of stones. ¾ mile N.E. of (6).

(8) **An Gearanach** (3200 feet)=the wall-like ridge. ⅓ mile N. of (9).

(9) **An Garbhanach** (3200 feet)=the rough ridge. ⅓ mile N.N.E. of (7).

(10) **Na Gruagaichean** (3442 feet)=the maidens. 2½ miles N.E. of Kinlochleven.

(11) Na Gruagaichean, N.W. top (3404 feet). ¼ mile N.W. of (10).

(12) **Binnein Mòr** (3700 feet)=the great hill. 1 mile N.N.E. of (10).

(13) Binnein Mòr, S. top (3475 feet). ½ mile S. of (12).

(14) **Binnein Beag** (3083 feet)=the little hill. 1 mile N.N.E. of (12).

(15) Sgùrr Eilde Beag (3140 feet)=the little crag of the hinds. ½ mile S.E. of (13).

(16) **Sgùrr Eilde Mòr** (3279 feet)=the big crag of the hinds. 1 mile N. of Loch Eilde Mòr.

As will be understood, this district is well adapted for ridge wandering, and numerous delightful circuits can be made. The ridge is mostly above the 2750-foot contour, and only in three places does it drop below 2500 feet, namely, between (3) and (5), 2450 feet ; between (12) and (14), 2400 feet approx. ; and between (15) and (16), 2400 feet approx.

These mountains with the exception of Mullach nan Coirean, which is granite, are of mica-schist and quartzite, so common in the Central Highlands. It is a hard and crystalline rock, and breaks up into angular fragments forming loose screes on the upper slopes. The uniform texture of the rock does not favour the formation of craggy features, and smooth, rounded hills crowned with conical summits are the result. The white quartzite is often mistaken for snow, as, for instance, in the cases of Sgùrr a' Mhaim and Stob Bàn, the upper slopes of which are almost white in certain lights. The name of the latter, of course, means " the white mountain."

Mullach nan Coirean (3077 feet).—This is probably the flattest and most uninteresting hill of the group. The summit plateau above the 2750-foot contour is very extensive, and the south top (3004 feet), denoted by a small contour, is very difficult to find in misty weather. The main top is more defined, and its north and east ridges are useful landmarks. Almost everywhere the slopes are covered with grass, and the scree slopes so common on the other tops are absent here. The mountain can be ascended easily from all sides, but the old Fort William-Loch Leven road is the most convenient route.

Stob Bàn (3274 feet).—This is a beautiful cone-shaped mountain with a distinctive quartzite top. It is one of the features of the view up Glen Nevis. The usual line of ascent is from Polldubh in Glen Nevis up the north ridge. This ridge has a very prominent top (2950 feet), about $\frac{1}{3}$ mile short of the summit, and this may easily be mistaken for the real summit in bad weather. Another route is by the old Fort William road to the watershed (1100 feet) at Tigh-na-sleubhaich. From here a direct climb may be made up the south-west ridge. The quartzite screes at the top are, however, very bad.

There is a path up the Allt Coire a' Mhusgain to the saddle between Stob Bàn and Sgòr an Iubhair, which gives a good line of approach to both these hills. The path goes up under the south ridge of Sgùrr a' Mhaim and descends on the south of the saddle almost to the old road.

The north-east face of Stob Bàn is precipitous, and there is some rock-climbing to be had on the three main buttresses.

The north buttress was climbed in April 1895 by Tough, Brown, Douglas, and Hinxman. Apparently many of the better pitches could have been avoided, but the route taken gave a good climb and finished on the lower north top.

The central buttress has a very steep triangular lower face. The slanting ridge to the left of this, between two gullies, was climbed in January 1904 by J. Maclay and Parr. The rocks were slabby and sloping outwards, and 1½ hours were taken for the 200 feet to the top of the lower buttress. From here to the summit ridge was easy.

The south or summit buttress is directly under the summit. It is split by a very obvious gully just to the south of the summit and is separated from the central buttress by another conspicuous gully. This summit buttress was explored by Currie, Henderson Scott and Anderson (all S.M.C.), and by Allison and Black (J.M.C.S.) in April 1948. The obvious gully proved to be quite easy, but a good route was worked out starting at the foot of the buttress and going up 150 feet of steep and difficult rock and finishing a few yards from the summit cairn. Allison and Black did a more difficult variation to the left on the lower steep rocks.

The same party also glissaded the conspicuous gully between the summit buttress and the central buttress.

All these gullies and buttresses are clearly shown in the photograph (p. 112-113).

Sgùrr a' Mhaim (3601 feet).—This is the second highest top in the Mamores. Its huge mass fills up the head of Glen Nevis, and its beautiful little cup-shaped north corrie is a conspicuous feature in the view south from Ben Nevis. The usual line of ascent is from Polldubh up the north-west ridge. If one descends by the north-east ridge towards Steall it should be remembered that the old cottage now in ruins on the right bank of the Nevis has had its name transferred to the keeper's cottage on the left bank. There is a wire bridge across the Nevis here just above the head of the gorge.

If the ascent is made from Steall a more interesting route than the N.E. ridge will be found by cutting south across the little N.E. corrie to the east ridge. This gives a good scramble of 800 feet up to a rocky pinnacle near the main N.E. ridge. From here to the summit the ridge is narrow.

The south ridge is sometimes called the Devil's Ridge. Under heavy snow it has quite a formidable appearance, but nowhere is it more than an exhilarating walk. About ½ mile

along the ridge there is a small shapely peak, unnamed but
marked by a 3250-foot contour. This is now known as
Stob Coire a' Mhail.

Sgòr an Iubhair (3300 feet).—This top stands at the
junction of the Sgùrr a' Mhaim south ridge and the main
ridge. It is not marked on the one-inch map, but it is denoted
by a small 3250-foot contour.

Am Bodach (3382 feet).—This peak is well seen from
Loch Leven, but the finest view of it is from Sgùrr a' Mhaim.
From the saddle to the west (2800 feet) a path runs down
into Coire na h-Eirghe, crossing to the right bank of the
stream at about 2400 feet and continuing down to the old
road about 2 miles from Kinlochleven.

Kinlochleven is the best centre for all peaks from Am
Bodach eastwards. A private driving road runs from the
old Fort William road past the Lodge (about 700 feet) to
Lochs Eilde Mòr and Beag. One path runs from the road
up into Coire na Ba. Another path runs from the road
½ mile west of Loch Eilde Mòr, north-east up to the saddle
between the south top of Binnein Mòr and Sgùrr Eilde Beag.
A branch from this path contours round to the bealach, with
the lochans west of Sgùrr Eilde Mòr. The path from Kinlochleven to the old Fort William road branches off the main
road just east of the loch and runs north-west, crossing the
lower part of the new private road to the Lodge.

Stob Coire a' Chairn (3219 feet).—This peak is unnamed
on the one-inch map, but it stands at the junction of the
An Garbhanach ridge and the main ridge. The col to the
south-west is about 2800 feet, and to the south-east, 2555 feet.
Both these saddles are crossed by the paths coming up from
the Allt Coire na Ba.

An Gearanach (3200 feet).—This is the north end of a
well-defined wall-like ridge which runs for about 600 yards
south to **An Garbhanach** (3200 feet). It would appear that
the northerly summit is the higher of the two. The ridge
between is exceptionally narrow for a grassy ridge, but only
rocky at its southern end. From the saddle to the south
(2800 feet) An Garbhanach presents a fine, bold, rocky
appearance, but the rocks are too broken up and indefinite
to provide any real climbing. The descent to Steall is by

the N.W. ridge, and the Nevis is crossed by a wire bridge just below the cottage.

Na Gruagaichean (3442 feet).—This is the second highest point on the main ridge. It is a rather featureless mountain with two tops only $\frac{1}{4}$ mile apart. The best route is to take the path up Coire na Ba to the bealach (2555 feet) north-west of the lower top, and from there follow the ridge over both tops and descend by the south ridge to the road. There is a dip of 200 feet between the two tops.

Binnein Mòr (3700 feet).—This is the highest mountain in the Mamore forest and also the most outstanding. From the north and from the south it appears as a graceful sharp-pointed peak ; from the east and from the west it rises up as a great clean-cut ridge. The summit ridge runs north and south for $\frac{1}{2}$ mile, with the south top (3475 feet) at one end and the main top at the other. Steep slopes of quartzite screes run down on all sides. The south top is on the main ridge and is the highest point on that ridge. The saddle to the S.W. is about 3100 feet. The best route of ascent is over Na Gruagaichean, or over the col between the two tops of that mountain and along the ridge to the 3475 feet top. A longer route, but probably more often used, is the one from Steall in Glen Nevis which leads up the N.N.W. ridge. Another good route from the south is to take the path referred to above leading up to the saddle S.E. of the south top.

Binnein Beag (3083 feet).—This is a very perfect cone-shaped little hill with steep quartzite screes on all sides. It is usually climbed from Glen Nevis by parties *en route* for its big brother, Binnein Mòr. The saddle between the two hills is 2400 feet.

Sgùrr Eilde Beag (3140 feet).—This is a very doubtful top, as the drop between it and the south top of Binnein Mòr is almost imperceptible. The path which runs up from Coire na Laogh to this N.W. saddle is an easy means of approach. The eastern slopes of the mountain are steep and lead down some 750 feet to a broad saddle with one large and several small lochans. The path above referred to branches and contours round to the west of the lochans and leads over to the Allt Coire a' Bhinnean, the head-waters of the Nevis.

Sgùrr Eilde Mòr (3279 feet).—This is a broad flat-topped mountain, like Mullach nan Coirean at the other end of the range. It can be climbed easily from the road at Loch Eilde Mòr (1122 feet). The northern ridge is broad and slopes gently down towards the watershed between the Nevis and the Amhainn Rath which flows down to Loch Treig. The ridge ends in a conspicuous top, Meall Doire na h-Achlais (2150 feet), and is sometimes followed by parties going from Corrour to Fort William who wish to add at least one mountain to their day's walk.

GLEN NEVIS

The River Nevis is about 14 miles long. It rises on the eastern slopes of Binnein Mòr and flows west and north-west to fall into the head of Loch Linnhe, near Fort William. Glen Nevis is one of the most beautiful glens in Scotland. In its higher reaches it is open, desolate moorland, between mountains possessing no very outstanding features as viewed from the glen. Passing from this more or less commonplace portion, it becomes, without any intervening change in scenery, the wildest and most magnificent gorge in the whole country. Below Steall cottage the southern buttresses of Ben Nevis project into the glen and meet the steep rocky shoulder of Sgùrr a' Mhaim, apparently shutting off all egress from the upper glen. Through this rocky rampart the wild stream has carved out its tortuous course, while high above on the right bank runs a rocky path, guarded by wire ropes and iron stanchions, which leads from the desolate moors around Steall to the sylvan beauty of the lower glen. The Nevis gorge is about 1 mile in length, and from its lower end there is a driving road to Fort William (7 miles) through the open glen. The road crosses to the left bank in 2 miles just above the farm of Polldubh. The whole stretch from the gorge to the sea is through charming pastoral and wooded country. The gradients are negligible, as the top of the road just below the gorge is only 450 feet above sea-level. Incidentally the slope leading from here to the summit of Ben Nevis directly above must be the longest and steepest in the country, 4000 feet at an average angle of over 35 degrees.

The views looking up Glen Nevis are specially fine, with the huge bulk of Sgùrr a' Mhaim at the head flanked on the right by the graceful peak of Stob Bàn.

The driving road up the glen is a useful line of approach to the Mamore Forest group, and, in addition, from Steall one can reach the Aonachs and the Easains up the Allt Coire Giubhsachan, or by the stream coming down from Chòinnich Beag. As already indicated, from the head of the road a steep scramble of 4000 feet leads directly up to the summit of Ben Nevis (4406 feet). Coming over the Aonachs from the north, or over the Grey Corries (Easains) from Spean Bridge, one can hope for a cup of tea at Steall or Polldubh and arrange for a motor at the foot of the gorge.

Steall Cottage (which formerly referred to the ruined cottage on the right bank of the Nevis) is situated on the left bank of the Nevis just above the gorge. It belongs to the Lochaber Section of the Junior Mountaineering Club of Scotland, and will accommodate at least nine climbers. There are Primus Stoves but no fuel. Access is gained to it by a wire-rope bridge which crosses the river just as the path emerges from the Nevis gorge.

In addition to providing a means of access to the hills, Glen Nevis is also a through route from Fort William to Loch Treig head and Corrour Station on the West Highland Railway. The distance is about 22 miles. As the expedition is usually made from Corrour to Fort William a short description of the route is given in that direction. A good track leads from the station down to Loch Treig. As the Loch has now been raised, go S.W. to Staoineag, 2½ miles, where there are stepping stones to the left bank of the Amhainn Rath and the path followed past the Lodge for about 4 miles. At Luibeilt the path crosses to the right bank and loses itself in the flat lands round the isolated hillock of Tom an Eite near the highest point of the route (1250 feet). On reaching the Nevis watershed the track keeps at first near the right bank of the stream and then cuts across to avoid the right angle where the Allt Coire na Gabhalach comes in on the left. From here to the head of the gorge it keeps about 300 yards to the right of the stream. If one wants to avoid the precipitous path through the gorge there is an alternative route which goes higher up and passes above the steep cliffs.

This is a very fine expedition, but if possible reasonably good weather should be chosen, as the section from Luibeilt to Steall is very heavy going and practically trackless.

LOWER GLEN NEVIS
Sgùr a' Mhaim on left and Stob Bàn on right.

J. R. Young

STOB COIRE A' CHAIRN, AN GARBHANACH, AND AN GEARANACH
From Binnein Mor.

April 1914

J. R. Young

SGÒR AN IUBHAIR AND STOB COIRE A' MHAIL.
From the Devil's Ridge.

THE CÀRN MÒR DEARG *ARÊTE*
Looking across Glen Nevis to Sgùrr a' Mhàim and Stob Bàn

March 1924

XIII

CÀRN MÒR DEARG

THIS mountain lies directly to the east of its famous neighbour Ben Nevis, and owes its popularity to the fact that the view from its crest of the great line of Nevis cliffs is the most striking panorama to be seen in this country. The tops are as follows :—

(1) **Càrn Mòr Dearg** (4012 feet) = the great red hill. ¾ mile N.E. of Ben Nevis.

(2) Càrn Dearg Meadhonach (3873 feet) = the middle red hill. ½ mile N.N.W. from (1).

(3) Càrn Beag Dearg (3264 feet) = the little red hill. 1 mile N.N.W. from (1).

The usual route for the ascent of all these tops is from the distillery on the Fort William-Inverness road about 2¼ miles from Fort William. There appears to be a right-of-way through the distillery grounds and so by the old Banavie-Ben Nevis path up into the Glen of the Allt a' Mhuilinn. Easy slopes lead from the glen up the N.W. slopes to the first top, Càrn Beag Dearg, which is really only a shoulder, and thereafter a delightful walk of a mile along the ridge takes one over Càrn Dearg Meadhonach to the cairn of Càrn Mòr Dearg. The ascent from the glen direct to the summit is not advisable, as the slopes are very steep and covered with unstable screes.

The ridge falls steeply on the east into the Allt Daimh, the head-waters of which rise in the saddle connecting Càrn Mòr Dearg with the Aonachs. There is an Ordnance Survey height on this saddle of 2915 feet, but this obviously does not refer to the saddle, which is plainly shown as lower than the 2750-foot contour. The height appears to be about 2700 feet.

The East Buttress of Carn Dearg Meadhonach consists of a rocky ridge descending to the Allt Daimh from the summit cairn. It is marked by a prominent pinnacle at about two-thirds of its height (summit of the pinnacle estimated 3800 feet) and a cluster of teeth further down at about 3700 feet. These, and particularly the former, are striking as seen in profile from Càrn Beag Dearg.

The upper pinnacle can be reached from the cairn of Càrn Dearg Meadhonach by descending a steep slope and then broken rocks to a small col, from which an ascent of about 20 feet over very rotten rock leads to the summit of the pinnacle.   This ascent involves only easy scrambling. The ascent of the whole Buttress appears to present no special difficulties other than those occasioned by the looseness of the rock.   The ascent to the higher pinnacle from the cluster of teeth is much less formidable than it appears from Carn Beag Dearg.

The well-known Càrn Mòr Dearg *arête*, which connects this mountain with Ben Nevis, is a very fine ridge affording some rock-scrambling.   The saddle drops to 3478 feet, so that the ascent to Ben Nevis from the ridge is nearly 1000 feet.

The ascent of Càrn Mòr Dearg is usually combined with that of Ben Nevis, and one of the finest high-level walks in the country is over the tops of Càrn Mòr Dearg along the *arête* and home over the summit of Ben Nevis.

The Charles Inglis Clark Memorial Hut, of course, provides a very convenient base for the ascent, lying as it does at a height of 2200 feet, less than ¾ mile due west of the cairn. The mountain may also be approached from Steall in Glen Nevis (see p. 96) up the Allt Coire Giubhsachan to the saddle connecting it with the Aonachs and then 1300 feet up the well-defined grassy ridge to the summit.

XIV

THE AONACHS (AONACH MÒR AND AONACH BEAG)

THESE two mountains are the culminating points of a long ridge, which runs almost north and south between Glen Spean and Glen Nevis and are easily climbed from either glen. Aonach Beag is about 2 miles directly east of the summit of Ben Nevis, and Aonach Mòr is about one mile north of Aonach Beag. Aonach Beag is the higher of the two (4060 feet as against 3999 feet), but it is sharper and less massive, and this accounts for the apparent anomaly in the names.

The principal summits are :

(1) **Aonach Mòr** (3999 feet) = the great height (? ridge).

(2) Stob an Cul Choire (3580 feet) = the peak at the back of the corrie. ⅔ mile E. by N. of (1).

(3) Stob Coire an Fhir Dhuibh (3250 feet approx.) = the peak of the corrie of the black man. 1 mile N.E. of (1).

(4) Tom na Sròine (3015 feet) = the hill of the nose. ½ mile N. of (3)

(5) **Aonach Beag** (4060 feet) = the little height (? ridge). 1 mile S. by E. of (1).

(6) Stob Coire Bhealaich (3644 feet) = the peak of the saddle. ½ mile S.E. of (5).

(7) Sgùrr a' Bhuic (3165 feet) = the peak of the buck. 1 mile S.E. by S. of (5).

On the west the Aonachs are connected with Càrn Mòr Dearg by a ridge which starts about midway between the Mòr and the Beag, and while it is not clearly marked against the Aonachs it develops into a well-defined ridge at its central part. The west side of the main ridge is fairly steep, while the east side is precipitous.

The ridge running S.E. from Aonach Beag has, in addition to Stob Coire Bhealaich, a fine top or buttress ½ mile farther on, where the ridge turns sharply to the south. This buttress rises steeply from the saddle connecting it on the east with Sgùrr Chòinnich Beag to an approximate height of 3500 feet, or 1100 feet above the saddle, and presents a very imposing appearance from below.

Aonach Mòr (3999 feet).—This is a very bulky and imposing ridge, rather like one of the Cairngorms. It is most easily approached from the old Fort William-Spean Bridge road from a point about 2 miles from the west end of the road. A bee-line is made for the broad north ridge, keeping Sgùrr Finnisg-aig on the left. The remains of a light railway will be crossed about the 1000-foot contour, and another 1000-foot rise will bring the climber into a very shallow corrie with the ridge, Aonach an Nid, on the left. This gently sloping corrie facing north usually carries plenty of snow and is admirably suited for ski-ing. Above 3500 feet the slope eases off, and thereafter the rise is almost imperceptible for $\frac{3}{4}$ mile to the very conspicuous summit cairn.

Stob an Cul Choire (3580 feet).—To reach this subsidiary top one goes due east from the cairn of Aonach Mòr to the edge of the more or less continuous line of cliffs on the east already referred to. A little to the left will be found the way down to the ridge which leads to the Stob and the other outlying tops on this north-east ridge.

Stob Coire an Fhir Dhuibh (3250 feet).—A short descent and a rise of about 50 feet places one on this second top.

Tom na Sròine (3015 feet).—This name on the map is applied to the termination of the ridge at the 2000-foot contour, but is here used for the second top enclosed in the 3000-foot contour a little more than $\frac{1}{2}$ mile north of Fhir Dhuibh. It is quite a distinct little summit, well separated from the other tops on this ridge.

Aonach Beag (4060 feet).—The best route to this hill is to motor 9 miles from Fort William to the entrance to the gorge of Glen Nevis, walk through the gorge to Steall, and then make a bee-line for the summit cairn up the tributary of the Allt Coire Giubhsachan. Or the course of this main burn may be followed to near the saddle connecting Càrn Mòr Dearg with the Aonachs, and then turning east to the saddle between the Aonachs (3600 feet), a steep little climb up the N.W. ridge of Aonach Beag leads easily to the cairn.

Aonach Beag is an imposing looking mountain. It rises with fine sweeping lines from the south to form a great dome, the north side of which is cut away to form a line of cliffs overlooking the head-waters of the Allt a' Chùl Choire. The saddle connecting it with Aonach Mòr is narrow, and the first 100 feet up to Aonach Beag are steep and rocky, and might give considerable trouble to a party descending under winter conditions in misty weather.

The top is flat, with two very small cairns near the edge of the cliffs. The westerly cairn appears to be the actual top.

The North-East Ridge of Aonach Beag is the only rock-climb of any note. Like so many other climbs in Scotland, its possibilities were first noted by Professor Norman Collie. The actual exploration and first climb were done by Maclay, Naismith, and Thomson in April 1895. The only other recorded ascents were by Raeburn and the Inglis Clarks in April 1904 and by B. P. Kellet's party in August 1942. Its immunity from attack is due no doubt to its remoteness, as the ridge is well worth a visit. It rises from, roughly, the 2500-foot contour as a well-defined ridge, and runs up to the summit plateau at 4000 feet, about 60 yards to the N.W. of the cairn. At a height of about 3000 feet the ridge becomes a narrow rocky *arête*, and this continues for about 500 feet ; thereafter it becomes broader and easier as it approaches the summit. The narrow part in the middle for about 130 feet is the most sensational of any of the great ridges outside of Skye. It is, however, so well broken up that there should be no great difficulties except under severe winter conditions. It is possible to walk on to the ridge from the corrie on the east at 3000 feet, and again about 3600.

The ridge is very conspicuous to anyone approaching from the N.E. up the valley of the Cour. The head-waters of the Cour are successively known as the Allt Coire an Eòin and the Allt a' Chùl Choire. The ridge springs practically from the lip of the upper corrie lying below the Aonach Beag-Aonach Mòr saddle, out of which flows the Chùl Choire Burn.

Stob Coire Bhealaich (3644 feet).—A walk of ½ mile S.E. from Aonach Beag with a very small rise brings one to this top. This is one of the doubtful tops in Munro's Tables, and it has been suggested that the buttress already referred to at the end of the ridge overlooking the saddle to Sgùrr Chòinnich Beag should have the honour transferred to it.

Sgùrr a' Bhuic (3165 feet).—This top lies about ⅔ mile south of the above unnamed buttress, and the saddle between them is about 2960 feet. This is a shapely peak and conspicuous from many points to the east.

XV

THE GREY CORRIES

UNDER the above title—an old local name and most descriptive—are included the two groups of hills lying between Glen Spean and Glen Nevis, and extending westwards from Loch Treig to the Aonachs. The two groups are separated by a deep depression through which runs the Lairig Leacach from the head of Loch Treig in a north-westerly direction to Spean Bridge. This track runs from near Creaguaineach Lodge up the right bank of the Allt na Lairige to within one mile of the water-shed, where it becomes a hill road. The track is only a rough sheep path and entirely disappears from time to time. The Lairig Leacach is the best route to these groups from Spean Bridge or from Corrour Station. On the north side of these hills the old Spean Bridge-Fort William road gives an approach to the western summits. The south-west end of the group is best reached from Steall in Glen Nevis (see p. 96).

The west group is the more important and comprises the following :—

(1) **Stob Choire Claurigh** (3858 feet) = (meaning obscure). 4½ miles S. of Roy Bridge.

(2) Stob Choire Claurigh, north top (3719 feet). ⅓ mile N. of (1).

(3) Stob Coire Gaibhre (3150 feet) = the peak of the corrie of the goats. 1¼ miles N. of (1).

(4) Stob Coire na Ceannain (3720 feet) = the peak of the corrie of the bluff. ¼ mile N.E. of (2).

(5) Stob a' Choire Lèith (3627 feet) = the peak of the steep-sided corrie. ⅓ mile W. by S. of (1).

(6) **Stob Bàn** (3217 feet) = the white peak. 1 mile S. by E. of (1).

(7) **Stob Coire an Laoigh** (3659 feet) = the peak of the corrie of the calf. 1¼ miles S.W. of (5).

(8) Stob Coire an Easain (3545 feet) = the peak of the corrie of the waterfall. ¼ mile N.W. of (7).

(9) Caisteal (3609 feet) = the castle. ¼ mile N.E. of (7).

(10) Stob Coire Cath na Sine (3529 feet) = the peak of the corrie of the battle of storm. ½ mile E. by N. of (9).

(11) **Sgùrr Chòinnich Mòr** (3603 feet) = the big rocky crag of the moss. ¾ mile S.S.W. of (8).

(12) Sgùrr Chòinnich Beag (3175 feet) = the little rocky crag of the moss. ½ mile S.W. of (11).

Access to these hills being difficult in summer and autumn, they are mostly climbed in spring, when under snow, and they are much better adapted for snow-work than rock-climbing, as, with the exception of the north face of Caisteal, which is precipitous, there seems little else bounding the ridges than steep slopes. In spring this group certainly offers the opportunity for one magnificent ridge walk of about 5 miles in length, which should in early spring be entirely over snow. For this excursion either Spean Bridge or Roy Bridge are convenient starting-points, and a car can be taken up the Lairig Leacach road past Corriecoillie to the bend in the road at the 800-foot contour. Here the climber is confronted by the magnificent snow-lined Coire Gaibhre, up whose steep slopes he will perhaps select a sporting route or he may go farther on and start the ridge with Stob Coire na Ceannain.

From Stob Coire na Ceannain the ridge is somewhat narrow to the north peak of Stob Choire Claurigh, after which it widens out and winds onward from one summit to another in a decidedly commonplace manner, although the descent from Stob Coire an Easain is rather rocky and broken up. The walk along the ridge thus affords no climbing ; its features, if taken in this direction, are the magnificent views obtained ahead of the Aonachs and Ben Nevis and the eastern peaks of the Mamore Forest.

All the tops can be climbed in this walk, with the exception of Stob Bàn, which lies off the main ridge, and the ridge can be left at Sgùrr Chòinnich Beag and a S.W. course steered direct to Steall in Glen Nevis (see p. 96).

An alternative walk would be from Loch Treig head, reached from Corrour Station, up the Lairig Leacach to Stob Bàn. From here the route would lie north to Stob Choire Claurigh and on to Stob Coire Gaibhre and Spean Bridge, or, by contouring round N.W., the saddle between Stob a' Choire Lèith and Stob Coire Cath na Sine could be reached and the walk continued to Chòinnich Beag and Steall.

Another variation is to leave the main ridge at Stob Coire an Easain and go north along the ridge to Beinn na Socaich and down the beautiful Cour glen to Spean Bridge. A track will be found on the east side of the Cour from Coire Coillie, crossing to the left bank before the junction with the Allt

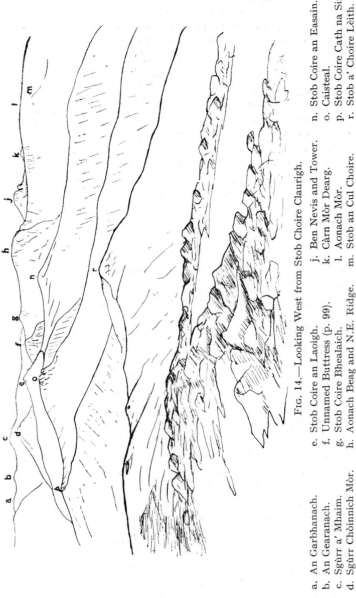

Fig. 14.—Looking West from Stob Choire Claurigh.

a. An Garbhanach.
b. An Gearanach.
c. Sgùrr a' Mhaim.
d. Sgùrr Chòinnich Mòr.
e. Stob Coire an Laoigh.
f. Unnamed Buttress (p. 99).
g. Stob Coire Bhealaich.
h. Aonach Beag and N.E. Ridge.
j. Ben Nevis and Tower.
k. Càrn Mòr Dearg.
l. Aonach Mòr.
m. Stob an Cul Choire.
n. Stob Coire an Easain.
o. Caisteal.
p. Stob Coire Cath na Sine.
r. Stob a' Choire Lèith.

P. Donald

LOOKING WEST FROM STOB CHOIRE CLAURIGH

(see Fig. 14 for details)

THE PARALLEL ROADS OF GLEN ROY

an Loin. Another route to Spean Bridge is by a track which starts at the Cour about the 600-foot contour below Coire Lianachain woods and leads north to the old road at Lianachain.

The approaches to this group from the south, except from Steall, are bad, as the track up the Amhainn Rath from Loch Treig head and the path in Glen Nevis above Steall are very poor and difficult to follow (see p. 96).

The eastern group consists of the following :—

(1) **Stob Coire Easain** (3658 feet) = the peak of the corrie of the waterfalls. 1½ miles W. of Loch Treig.

(2) **Stob a' Choire Mheadhoin** (3610 feet) = the peak of the middle corrie. ⅔ mile N.E. of (1).

(3) Meall Cian Dearg (2500 feet approx.) = the long red hill. 1½ miles N.N.E. of (2).

(4) Sgùrr Innse (2500 feet approx.) = the rocky peak of the meadow. 1½ miles N.W. of (1).

This group consists of the double-topped mountain, whose south peak is Stob Coire Easain, the culminating point, and whose north peak is Stob a' Choire Mheadhoin. The main ridge runs N.N.E. from near Loch Treig head and is bounded on the east by Loch Treig and on the west by the Lairig Leacach. Meall Cian Dearg is the northern spur which overlooks Tulloch and provides the usual route to the higher summits farther south. Sgùrr Innse is a most remarkable-looking little hill, very steep on all sides. It rises precipitously for 1000 feet above the summit of the Lairig Leacach. Its steep rocky slopes would appear to offer considerable scope for rock-scrambling, if nothing better. The easiest route will be found on the northern slopes, which are less rocky than the others.

The route from Tulloch Station is by Inverlair, which is reached by going down the Roy Bridge road for a mile and then crossing over the railway and the Spean by a bridge. From Inverlair a track runs up the Allt Làire high above the left bank. At a height of 1000 feet a foot-bridge crosses the burn and gives access to the N.W. slopes of Meall Cian Dearg.

Thereafter the main ridge is followed first to Stob a' Choire Mheadhoin and then, after a dip of 600 feet, to Stob Coire Easain, on which will be found a well-made cairn. The N.W. corrie between the two peaks is fairly steep and

H

usually carries lots of snow. The whole ridge rises very steeply from the dark waters of Loch Treig.

From Corrour Station and Loch Treig head the Lairig Leacach can be followed to the 1250-foot contour and then a direct line made for the top of Stob Coire Easain. As this path is so bad, however, it would probably be just as easy to start right up the slopes from Loch Treig, and, leaving Creagan a' Chase on the right, climb up the long southern shoulder, Irlick Chaoile, to the summit.

THE PARALLEL ROADS OF GLEN ROY

In Glen Roy, Glen Spean, and Glen Gloy are to be found the well-known geological phenomena of the Parallel Roads. These shelves are now stated to be the remains of lake-shores and resemble the similar geological feature, raised sea-beaches, so common round our coasts. Dr. John Macculloch, in *The Highlands and Western Isles of Scotland*, 1824, refers to them, and was the first to suggest that they were lake-shores. The complete disappearance of the retaining barriers of the lakes, however, puzzled him greatly, and others too, until Agassiz put forward the theory of a dam caused by glacier ice choking the valley. In spite of this, the generally accepted theory now, Professor T. G. Bonney in his *Ice-work, Present and Past*, 1896, suggests that the disappearance of the dam was more probably due to submergence.

The Roads are in three tiers in Glen Roy, at average heights of 855 feet, 1067 feet, and 1148 feet. The only level apparent in Glen Gloy is 1165 feet and in Glen Spean 855 feet.

The ice-barrier of the 855-foot level lake was said to stretch from a point about one mile north of Spean Bridge, where a Parallel Road meets the Allt Odhar between the 700-foot and the 800-foot contours to a point S. by E. in the Cour valley at a height of 846 feet, where a Parallel Road approaches the Allt Choimhlidh, a tributary of the Cour.

XVI

THE LOCH TREIG HILLS

THIS group lies on the east side of Loch Treig and consists of the following :—

(1) **Chno Dearg** (3433 feet) = the red nut. 2 miles E. of Loch Treig and 4½ miles S.S.E. of Tulloch Station.

(2) Meall Garbh (3197 feet) = the rough rounded hill. ¾ mile S.W. by W. of (1).

(3) **Stob Coire Sgriodain** (3211 feet) = the peak of the scree corrie. 1½ miles W. of (1).

(4) Stob Coire Sgriodain, south top (3132 feet). ⅓ mile S.S.E. of (3).

These hills can all be most conveniently climbed by traversing them from Corrour Station to Tulloch Station or *vice versa*. From Corrour (1300 feet) the way lies N.W. either along the railway or the Loch Treig path until the Allt Luib comes in on the right at a height of 0125 feet. Crossing the burn, by the railway bridge if necessary, a slanting course is made up to the long ridge Garbh-bheinn, which runs down S.W. from Meall Garbh. From Meall Garbh, which has no cairn, a slight dip and gentle rise lead to Chno Dearg, the highest point of the group. A rather uninteresting tramp of 1½ miles, with a drop of 500 feet, leads to the south top of Stob Coire Sgriodain (no cairn). A descent of 200 feet and a gentle rise up a broad ridge leads to the north top. From this cairn the route is obvious—right down the north ridge over Sròn na Gàrbh-bheinne to Tulloch Station, 4 miles as the crow flies.

XVII

THE CORROUR HILLS

THE hills of the Corrour Forest form the western extension of that great mountain-shield whose central and culminating boss is Ben Alder, but are cut off from that mountain by the deep glens of the Bealach Dubh (Black Pass) and the Uisge Alder (Alder Water). The principal summits are as follows :—

- (1) **Beinn Eibhinn** (3611 feet)=the beautiful mountain. 3 miles N.E. of Loch Ossian.
- (2) Mullach Coire nan Nead (3025 feet)=height of the corrie of the nests. 1 mile W. of (1).
- (3) Uinneag a' Ghlas Choire (3041 feet)=the window of the grey corrie. ¾ mile W.S.W. of (1).
- (4) **Beinn na Lap** (3066 feet), (properly Lap Bheinn)=the boggy mountain. 2½ miles N.N.E. of Corrour Station.
- (5) Beinn Chumhainn (2958 feet)=the narrow ben. 1 mile N.N.E. of (6).
- (6) Meall a' Bhealaich (2827 feet)=hill of the pass. 1 mile N.E. of (7).
- (7) Sgòr Choinnich (3040 feet)=Kenneth's peak. ¾ mile N. of (8).
- (8) **Sgòr Gaibhre** (3128 feet)=peak of the goats. 2 miles E.N.E. of (10).
- (9) Beinn Pharlagain (2836 feet)=(meaning obscure). 2 miles S. of (8).
- (10) **Càrn Dearg** (3084 feet)=red cairn. 4 miles E. of Corrour Station.

Beinn Eibhinn (3611 feet), the highest point in the Corrour Forest, is only overtopped a few feet by its neighbour Aonach Beag, just across the forest march. The southern spurs of Beinn Eibhinn are comparatively featureless, but the mountain presents a bold front to the north and falls almost from the summit cairn in 1000 feet of crag and talus slope to the floor of Coire a' Chàrra Mhòir, a cirque of remarkable beauty and symmetry of form.

A steep grassy slope, strewn with granite blocks, leads westwards from the summit, with a fall of about 800 feet, to the high col which separates Beinn Eibhinn from the subsidiary peaks **Mullach Coire nan Nead** on the west and **Uinneag a' Ghlas Choire** on the south. On the rocky floor of the pass are two curious little tarns, lying close together, but at different levels, and draining in opposite directions. This top is only shown as in a 2750-foot contour on the old one-inch map. The mountain finally terminates abruptly in the precipitous eastern wall of Strath Ossian, where two great crags of ice-worn granite look down on either side over the green alluvial flats at the head of Loch Ghuilbinn, and form the portals of the glen. Each of these crags bears the name of Creagan nam Nead (Crags of the Nest), and have from time immemorial afforded a nesting site for the raven and the peregrine falcon.

From Corrour Station, where most trains can be stopped, there is a driving road to the Lodge, which was burned down some years ago, at the foot of Loch Ossian (4½ miles). From here the best route to Beinn Eibhinn is along the path from the Lodge to the foot-bridge crossing the Uisge Labhair, and then north up the long ridge overlooking Strath Ossian to the top of Mullach Coire nan Nead, from which the cairn on Beinn Eibhinn lies one mile due east. Another route is to continue up the path, after crossing the bridge, for a mile and then turn north up on to the ridge leading to Uinneag a' Ghlas Choire.

The view from Beinn Eibhinn is extremely fine, and there are few points from which the great elevated tableland, that extends in an almost unbroken line from Creag Meaghaidh to the northern limits of the Monadh Liadth, can be better observed. The outlook northwards to Loch Laggan and Strathspey is, however, blocked by the long ridge of Beinn a' Chlachair.

Beinn na Lap (3066 feet), the forest sanctuary, rises on the west side of Strath Ossian, with Loch Ossian lying under its southern slopes. It has some moderately good crags on the eastern face, but is otherwise uninteresting. It can be climbed easily from either end of Loch Ossian.

Beinn Chumhainn (2958 feet).—The five remaining hills on the list are the highest distinct tops of the long ridge which runs south-west and south from the western side of the Ben Alder massif, forming at once the march between the counties of Perth and Inverness, and the water parting between the Spean and the Tay—a part of the main watershed of Scotland.

The summits and western spurs of these hills are smooth and for the most part carpeted with crisp fringe-moss and alpine sedge, delightful to walk upon. The Perthshire side is, however, bold and rocky, and the granite slabs of Sgòr Choinnich and Sgòr Gaibhre, and the long scarp of broken crags of schist that looks down upon Glen Eigheach, might attract the attention of the rock-climber.

From Beinn Chumhainn, which presents a bold face to the N.E. above the head of the Uisge Alder Glen, the ridge runs for one mile S.S.W. to **Meall a' Bhealaich,** with an intervening drop of about 400 feet. The next col is considerably lower, the rise to the top of Sgòr Choinnich being at least 600 feet. The ridge now trends due south for ¾ mile to the summit of Sgòr Gaibhre, the highest point of the range, and thence 2 miles W.S.W. to Càrn Dearg. The fall to the saddle, Màm Bàn (2369 feet), from the former hill is 759 feet, and the rise to Càrn Dearg 715 feet, so it takes about one hour from top to top. From the last-named summit the ridge falls gradually to the S. by E. and terminates in Sròn Leachd a' Chaorruinn (2414 feet).

Sgòr Choinnich (3040 feet) is a fine steep hill with a most impressive corrie on its east side. The drop on the south ridge to the Bealach nan Sgòr is fully 400 feet, and this combined with its outstanding position almost entitles it to be classed as a separate mountain.

Sgòr Gaibhre (3128 feet).—The usual route from the Lodge is up the Allt a' Choire Chreagaich to its head, and thence to the Bealach nan Sgòr on the north side of the hill. The long south ridge runs for about 3½ miles, pursuing a serpentine course with many ups and downs over the tops of **Beinn Pharlagain** (2836 feet) to its southern buttress Leacann nan Giomach. This end of the ridge can be reached from Rannoch Station as explained below.

Càrn Dearg (3084 feet).—From Corrour Station the road should be followed to the loch, and then about 1½ miles farther east the moor should be crossed to the western shoulder of the mountain. This leads easily to the summit. The remains of the old Corrour Lodge track also provides a good approach to this western shoulder.

Càrn Dearg can also be approached from the south from Rannoch Station. A cycle, or even a car, can be taken up the old Corrour Lodge track (which leaves the Rannoch road 1½ miles E. of the station) as far as the ford over the Allt Eigheach, just past where the Allt Gormag comes in on the east. There is a turning-place here. If the eastern crags of the ridge are the object in view, the W. bank of this stream should now be taken ; a rough track follows the stream for about 2½ miles. To gain the Càrn Dearg ridge, follow the old Corrour Lodge track for 2 miles or so and then take the easiest line N.E. up the hill slope. Walkers can take a more direct route from the station along the railway for 1¼ miles and then strike N.N.E. across the peat moss (bad going) to the Corrour track. The distance from Rannoch Station to the top of Sròn Leachd a' Chaorruinn is about 4½ miles.

The Pharlagain ridge of Sgòr Gaibhre can also be reached from Rannoch Station. The track should be left at the ford over the Allt Eigheach and the left bank of the stream followed for ¾ mile before turning N.E. to gain the ridge.

XVIII

BEN ALDER GROUP

THIS magnificent group of mountains lies in the very heart of the Central Highlands, between Loch Ericht on the east, the Moor of Rannoch on the south and west, and Loch Laggan on the north. It falls naturally into three divisions; in the south Ben Alder proper, in the middle the great ridge running from Aonach Beag to Càrn Dearg, and in the north Beinn a' Chlachair and the other hills of the Ben Alder Forest.

The following are the principal tops :—

(1) **Ben Alder** (3757 feet) = the mountain of rock and water 12 miles from Dalwhinnie Station, and 10 miles from Corrour and Rannoch Stations.

(2) **Beinn Bheòil** (3333 feet) = the mountain in front (of Ben Alder). 1½ miles E. of (1).

(3) Sròn Coire na h-Iolaire (3128 feet) = nose of the eagles' corrie. ¾ mile S.S.W. of (2).

(4) **Aonach Beag** (3646 feet) = the little height (? ridge). 2¾ miles W.N.W. of (1).

(5) **Geal-Chàrn** (3688 feet) = the white cairn. 1 mile E.N.E. of (4).

(6) Sgòr Iutharn (3300 feet) = Hell's peak. 2 miles E. of (4).

(7) **Càrn Dearg** (3391 feet) = red cairn. 2½ miles N.E. of (5).

(8) Diollaid a' Chàirn (3029 feet) = the saddle of the cairn. 1 mile E.N.E. of (5).

(9) **Beinn a' Chlachair** (3569 feet) = the mason's mountain. 6 miles N. of (1).

(10) **Creag Pitridh** (3031 feet) = the rock of the hollow places. 4 miles S.S.W. of Ardverikie on Loch Laggan.

(11) **Mullach Coire an Iubhair** (3443 feet), (Geal Charn on 1-inch map) = the top of the corrie of the yew tree. 1 mile E. of (10).

(12) Sròn Garbh (3320 feet) = rough nose. ½ mile S. by E. of (11).

Ben Alder is a granite-capped mountain, the lower slopes being composed of the schistose rocks (chiefly gneiss) of the Central Highlands. The higher parts of the hill consist of a large summit plateau, containing no less than 380-400 acres of ground over 3500 feet. It plunges down in steep, rough corries—the Garracorries—to the Loch a' Bhealaich Bheithe on the east; on the north towards the Bealach Dubh and the head-waters of the Culrea it is fringed by a line of cliffs some 400 or 500 feet high; while to the west and south-west it slopes

J. R. Young

AM BODACH

112

B. H. Humble

NA GRUAGAICHEAN

STOB BAN

With Mullach nan Coirean to right and Beinn a' Bheithir and Loch Linnhe in background.

P. Donald

BINNEIN MÒR

J. R. Young

away easily towards the Uisge Alder. Beinn Bheòil and Sròn Coire na h-Iolaire are separated from Ben Alder by Loch a' Bhealaich Bheithe, and they lie between that mountain and Loch Ericht. They form a long ridge running parallel to the loch-side, sloping steeply towards the west, and more steeply, but seldom precipitously, to the east.

Ben Alder is somewhat difficult to get at. It is most easily reached from Dalwhinnie, where there is a good hotel. There is a driving road from Dalwhinnie for 6 miles along the north side of the loch to Loch Ericht Lodge. From the Lodge a private road runs west to Loch Pattack and then north to the east end of Loch Laggan. About a mile short of Loch Pattack a path goes off to the S.W. and runs up the Allt a' Chaoil-reidhe (the Culrea) to the Bealach Dubh (2300 feet) between Ben Alder and Geal-Chàrn. Then only dropping about 300 feet into the Uisge Labhair, it circles round the western slopes of Ben Alder and crosses the Bealach Cumhann and descends the Alder Burn (Uisge Alder) to within a few hundred yards of Ben Alder Cottage on Loch Ericht. Here again another path is picked up which leads N.E. along the shores of the loch back to the Lodge.

A subsidiary path leaves the Bealach Dubh path about 2½ miles short of the Bealach, goes in a southerly direction up to and along the east side of Loch a' Bhealaich Bheithe, terminating about ½ mile beyond the south side of the loch and 300 feet above it. This path is the usual route to Ben Alder from Dalwhinnie and the north. The eastern slopes of Ben Alder, which overlook the loch and the path, are very steep, but only in places are they rocky, and under good conditions they may be ascended almost anywhere.

For those who prefer a less steep ascent, the path to the Bealach Dubh should be followed to within ¾ mile of the saddle. Here a southerly course should be made up the stream which comes down from a steep little corrie. This lands one on the summit plateau about ¾ mile north of the cairn.

The long, narrow N.N.E. ridge which runs out on to the moor between the Bealach Dubh path and the subsidiary path gives a very picturesque and easy scramble to the summit plateau. It is the most direct route and is known as the Long Leachas. The shorter N.E. ridge about ½ mile south also gives an easy scramble and is known as the Short Leachas.

Another approach to Ben Alder is from Rannoch Station, but the two routes here involve considerable cross-country walks over boggy ground. Leaving Rannoch Station, walk east along the road for 1½ miles till the Corrour Lodge road is joined ; go along this north-west till you reach the Allt Gormag. Cross it, and then leaving the road, hold along past the north side of Lochan Sròn Smeur, keeping on the high south-eastern slopes of Beinn Pharlagain at a height of about 1250 feet. Cross the Cam Chriochan and go straight down to the loch-side and keep to it till you reach Ben Alder Cottage. If the day be bad, the burns high, and the moor very wet, this is the route to take. The other route is shorter, but as it necessitates the crossing of two large burns, and keeps more in the low-lying moor, it should only be taken if the weather be dry. Leaving Rannoch Station, walk east till the Corrour road is joined, then take to the hillside and go north-east over the southern slopes of Sròn Smeur. Cross the Allt Chaldar a full mile below the Lochan Lòin nan Donnlaich (the burn breaks away here among some rocks, making the crossing possible ; above that it is still and wide and deep). Continue along in the same direction (north-east), having Lochan Lòin nan Donnlaich on your left and Meall Liath na Doire Mhòir on your right, pass beside Lochan na h-Aon Chraoibh, and so to Loch Ericht side. A new bridge on the Cam Chriochan will be found about 100 yards from where it enters the loch. The burns all about here may give trouble when in spate, and the " going " over the moor is very heavy.

Perhaps the best route to Ben Alder from the south is from the west end of Loch Rannoch. A good path will be found starting from behind the sawmill and going north-west. It gradually turns north and circles round to the west of Meall Liath na Doire Mhòir (1624 feet). Where the path forks, the right branch is taken, and this leads down to the Cam Chriochan, which is crossed by the bridge. From here the path continues on through the remains of an old forest but stops abruptly about 1½ miles from Ben Alder Cottage.

Another route from Loch Rannoch is up the River Ericht by the new road built in connection with the dam at Loch Ericht. This is a private road, and permission must be obtained before motoring up it. The dam is just beyond where the Allt Ghlas comes in from the north-east. The road stops here, and the route then lies across the dam to the right bank, and then north-west over very bad ground to the Cam Chriochan.

Ben Alder Cottage is no longer occupied, and owing to the extension of the loch following on the completion of the Grampian Water Scheme it is now fully 4 miles of very bad going from the south-west end of the loch to the cottage.

Ben Alder has some very interesting associations with Prince Charlie. Towards the close of his adventurous wanderings after Culloden, he, along with some followers, on 29th August 1746, reached " Corrineuir," *i.e.*, Coire an Iubhair. They then moved on to " Mellaneuir," *i.e.*, Meallan Odhar, beside Loch Pattack, and after a day to " Uiskchilra," *i.e.*, the Culrea (Gaelic, Uisge Chaoil Reidhe), " two miles further into Ben Alder to a little shiel . . . superlatively bad and smokey." There they stayed for two or three nights, when they moved " two miles further into the mountain to Cluny's Cage in the face of a very rough, high rocky mountain, which is still a part of Ben Alder." In this Cage, along with Cluny, Lochiel, and others, he spent a week. As the Cage, was a perishable structure composed of boughs and moss, and built into a holly tree in the face of a cliff, manifestly " Prince Charlie's Cave," just above the keeper's house, cannot be it nor even the site of it. The Cage was probably constructed somewhere in the rocky corrie which faces the loch about half a mile north-east of Alder Bay, and the present " cave " is the concrete embodiment of the tradition of the Cage of old Cluny Macpherson.

Beinn Bheòil (3333 feet) is a rather uninteresting hill made up of a long regular ridge running for 2 miles parallel to Loch Ericht. On its westerly side very steep scree slopes run down to the valley of Loch a' Bhealaich Bheithe. The Loch Ericht slopes are also steep, an average angle of over 30 degrees, but they are grassier.

Sròn Coire na h-Iolaire (3128 feet) is the southern end of the ridge and is quite a distinct top. Below this top on the west the Bealach Breabag (2700 feet) connects with the south-east shoulder of Ben Alder.

Aonach Beag (3646 feet) is the west top of a great

mountain plateau which rivals Ben Alder in size.   To the
north-west and south-south-west quite distinct ridges run
out, but to the east the slope falls gradually for about 300 feet
before rising to merge into the great plateau of Geal-Chàrn.
The ridge to the south-west descends steeply for 500 feet
to the saddle connecting it with Beinn Eibhinn.   The usual
route of ascent is from Beinn Eibhinn or from Geal-Chàrn.

Geal-Chàrn (3688 feet) is the highest part of an extensive
plateau all above the 3500-foot contour.   The summit consists
of a " vast but shallow depression many acres in extent in
which a huge snow-field evidently deposits itself annually."
When this melts it leaves stretches of pasture-land, providing
excellent feeding ground for deer.   Geal-Chàrn has no name
or height on the one-inch map, but the summit is about
$\frac{1}{8}$ inch to the east of the name " Coire na Coichille."   There
is no cairn.   It is unfortunate that Geal-Chàrn is higher than
Aonach Beag and that both have established claims to be
treated as separate mountains.   As the higher, the former
can rightly claim the honour, but the latter is a more outstanding top and it is no doubt due to its appearance that
its subservience to Geal-Chàrn has been overlooked !   The
usual route of ascent is from Aonach Beag or from Sgòr
Iutharn.

Sgòr Iutharn (3300 feet) is the summit of the well-known
Lancet Edge, the narrow, rocky eastern ridge of the Geal-
Chàrn plateau.   It is not named on the one-inch map, but
the top is shown by the small 3250-foot contour.   There is
no cairn.   Coming from Dalwhinnie direction by the path
already referred to (see p. 113), Lancet Edge is the obvious
route to Geal-Chàrn.   The Edge soon steepens and becomes
quite narrow, with rocky steps formed by the usual schistose
outcrops.   Except under snow conditions there is no difficulty,
but care is necessary for several hundred feet.   As the top
is approached, the slope on the left to the Bealach Dubh
becomes less steep, but precipitous rocks continue on the
right round above Lochan Sgòir.

Càrn Dearg (3391 feet) is the culminating point on the
long north-east ridge which runs out from the Geal-Chàrn
plateau.   It is usually climbed from Loch Pattack by the
path running south from the loch to the Culrea Burn or
from the path already described running up that stream

(see p. 113). The ascent can be conveniently combined with that of Geal-Chàrn.

Diollaid a' Chàirn (3029 feet) is an almost imperceptible rise in the ridge connecting Càrn Dearg with Geal-Chàrn. It is hard to justify its claim to be treated as a separate top. A well-defined ridge leads to the Geal-Chàrn plateau, and in misty weather it is not easy to hit off this ridge when coming from the west.

Beinn a' Chlachair (3569 feet).—This fine mountain is very isolated and difficult of access. It can be approached by a path from Loch Pattack passing north of Loch a' Bhealaich Leamhain, but probably the best route is from the Loch Laggan road at Moy up the Amhainn Ghuilbinn and by a path which strikes south by east over Meall Ardruigh to Lubvan and thence up the western slopes.

Creag Pitridh (3031 feet).—This is a prominent little mountain, one mile south-east of the southern half of Lochan na h-Earba. There is a private road through the Ardverikie estate from the north-east end of Loch Laggan right up to the head of the northern half of Lochan na h-Earba. Thereafter one path runs south-west along the southern half of the Lochan past Creag Pitridh at a height of 1160 feet, and another path runs south-east and circles round into the north corrie of Geal Charn (see below). From the first of these paths it is an easy climb of some 1900 feet to the cairn on Creag Pitridh. The west ridge is fairly well defined, but to the east the mountain slopes down gradually and merges into a broad boggy saddle (2600 feet) before rising to Geal Charn. A branch path from the second referred to above crosses this saddle and goes south to the saddle (2365 feet) between Beinn a' Chlachair and Geal Charn.

Mullach Coire an Iubhair (3443 feet), or **Geal Charn** as it appears on the one-inch map, is rather an imposing looking mountain, especially as seen from the flat ground to the east. It can be climbed from the Creag Pitridh direction or more conveniently from the Loch Pattack road. This private road can be reached from the Loch Laggan road, about 1½ miles east of the loch, by a foot-bridge over the Pattack or from Dalwhinnie by Loch Ericht (see p. 113). About 1½ miles north of Loch Pattack a path goes off to the west up the Allt a' Mheallain Odhair. This path turns slightly north of west and crosses below the north corrie of Geal Charn and joins the path from Lochan na h-Earba already referred to.   From this north corrie the summit plateau is easily reached, and the large well-made cairn will be found about 200 yards to the west.

Sròn Garbh (3320 feet).—This is the top indicated on the hill-shaded ordnance map at the junction of the north-east and south-east ridges.   The top is named on the six-inch map, but the height " 3206 " is merely a point on the north-east ridge about ⅓ mile beyond the actual top.

XIX

THE DRUMOCHTER HILLS

THE principal summits of this group are as follows :—

(1) **Sgairneach Mhòr** (3210 feet) = the big rocky hillside. 3 miles W. of Dalnaspidal Station.

(2) **Beinn Udlamain** (3306 feet) = the mountain of the unsteady place. 1 mile W. by N. of (1).

(3) **A'Mharconaich** (3185 feet) = (meaning obscure). 2 miles N.E. of (2).

(4) **Geal Chàrn** (3005 feet) = the white cairn. 4½ miles S.S.W. of Dalwhinnie.

(5) An Torc (2432 feet) = the Boar of Badenoch. 1¼ miles E. by N. of (3).

(6) The Sow of Athole (2500-foot contour). 1½ miles S. of (5).

This group, lying between Loch Ericht to the north-west, Loch Garry to the south-east, and the Perth-Inverness Railway over the Drumochter Pass to the east, forms a horseshoe round the grassy Coire Dhomhain, with Geal Chàrn as an outlier to the north. The whole of its smooth-topped summits can be traversed in a fairly easy walk, almost without retracing one's steps at all, and without much intermediate dip. The nearest hotel is at Dalwhinnie (1100 feet), which is 7 miles by road from Dalnaspidal (1350 feet). The usual traverse of the hills is from Dalnaspidal to Dalwhinnie or *vice versa*.

To the ordinary tourist the group is best known as including two hills called the Sow of Athole and the Boar of Badenoch (both of which are conspicuous from the railway and from the main road).

An Torc, or the Boar of Badenoch (2432 feet), rises by a very steep shoulder 950 feet above the railway, immediately to the west of the summit level at the county march ; while the " Sow of Athole "—Meall an Dobhrachan as it is called on the six-inch map—is the 2500-foot contour shown on the one-inch map, a short 1½ miles south of An Torc.

Sgairneach Mhòr (3210 feet).—From Dalnaspidal Station the route lies south-west past the cottages to the bridge over the Allt Dubhaig, and then up the Allt Coire Luidhearnaidh, keeping to the left bank until a north-west course leads up easy slopes to the top. The point marked 3160 on the one-inch map is ⅓ mile S.W. of the highest point, which is on the broad ridge running roughly east and west and marked by a small cairn. The summit appears to be at least 100 feet higher than the 3160 feet top. The northern slopes are fringed by a range of cliffs about 300 feet high overlooking Coire Creagach. There is also a good route up the Allt Coire Dhomhain by a path on the left bank reached from the main road about 1½ miles north of Dalnaspidal Station. From the minor summit (3160 feet) an excellent ski run goes down the little stream running due north into the Dhomhain valley, where it joins the path referred to above. The route to the **Sow of Athole** lies at first along the fairly well-defined ridge to the east and north-east, and then descends on to broad slopes leading up to the Sow. The highest point of the Sow is near the north end of the 2500-foot contour. A descent can be made down the easy south-east ridge and a direct line made for Dalnaspidal Station if the river is small, or for the bridge in times of flood.

To continue from Sgairneach Mhòr to **Beinn Udlamain** in misty weather is not quite simple, and the map is not very accurate. The best way is to go S.W. for 600 yards and then N.W. for 800 yards to the top marked 3053 feet, but not marked by a 3000-foot contour in the hill-shaded one-inch map. From here a descent of 400 feet in a south-westerly direction for ½ mile places one on the saddle. The maps here show the stream on the south crossing the bealach and rising on the north slopes about 150 feet lower and ¼ mile farther on ! From the saddle Beinn Udlamain (3306 feet) is reached by the south ridge.

From Udlamain the ridge runs N.N.E. for ½ mile to an unnamed top (3213 feet on the old one-inch map), and then N.E., dropping only to 2800 feet, to the great broad plateau of **A'Mharconaich** (3185 feet). The maps show a height of 3174 feet on the county boundary and a name Bruach nan Iomairean, but the highest point is ½ mile away, near the N.N.E. corner of the 3150-foot contour of the one-inch Popular Edition.

An Torc, or the **Boar of Badenoch** (2422 feet), is easily climbed if one is returning to the Drumochter Pass. The

THE CORRIEYAIRACK PASS

The bridge over the Allt Coire Uchdachan on the north side.

W. Lamond Howie

BEN ALDER GROUP

Beinn Bheòil on the left ; the flat top of Ben Alder and the Long Leachas ; the Bealach Dubh; Lancet Edge ;
Geal Chàrn behind, and on right Carn Dearg.

north and north-east slopes are steep, and the easiest way
down is by the south-east.

The route to **Geal Chàrn** (3005 feet) lies west from the
3174-foot top of A'Mharconaich over gently undulating
broad grassy slopes. The saddle here is 2426 feet. All these
slopes here are excellent for ski-running, and can be approached
from Dalwhinnie over the long N.E. ridge of Creagan Mòr
(2522 feet), an unnamed top (2507 feet), and Geal Chàrn itself.

Dalwhinnie is, of course, one of the best ski-ing centres
in Scotland, standing as it does at 1150 feet and served by
both road and rail. The hills all round are grassy, with easy
slopes, and if the Geal Chàrn group offers no inducement,
the slopes and great gullies to the east running up to Càrn
na Caim (3087 feet) may carry sufficient snow. The gorge
of the Allt Coire Uilleim, which runs from the summit plateau
down to where the road crosses the main stream, gives a
very fine ski run.

None of these mountains offers any attractions to the
rock-climber. The views, however, especially of the Ben
Alder group, are interesting, and as they are not in a deer
forest they are accessible at all seasons.

XX

CREAG MEAGHAIDH RANGE

THIS extensive group of rounded hills, of which Creag Meaghaidh (Craig Meggie) is the culminating point, lies between the upper Spey valley and Glen Roy on the north and west, and Glen Spean and Loch Laggan on the south. The north-eastern end of the range is very uniform in elevation, but towards the western end the summits are more marked. The chief characteristics of the hills are deep and precipitous corries, of which the best known is Coire Ardair (the corrie of the high wood).

The chief summits in the range are as follows :—

(1) **Beinn a' Chaoruinn** (3437 feet)=the mountain of the rowan tree. 3¼ miles N.N.E. of Tulloch Station.

(2) Beinn a' Chaoruinn, north top (3422 feet). ¾ mile N. by W. of (1).

(3) **Creag Meaghaidh** (3700 feet)=(meaning obscure). 2½ miles N.E. of (2).

(4) An Cearcallach (3250 feet)=the hoop. 1⅛ miles S. by E. of (3).

(5) Meall Coire Choille-rais (3299 feet)=the top of the corrie of the shrub wood. 1¼ miles S.E. of (3).

(6) Puist Coire Ardair (3591 feet)=the post of the high corrie. 1 mile E. of (3).

(7) Creag Mhòr (3496 feet)=the great rock. ½ mile E. of (6).

Separated from the above by the very marked bealach known as the Window (3200 feet) are the following seven summits, all lying on the long ridge running for about 6 miles E.N.E. These are as follows :—

(8) **Poite Coire Ardair** (3460 feet)=the pot of Corrie Arder. 1 mile N.N.E. of (3).

(9) Poite Coire Ardair, east top (3441 feet). ½ mile E.N.E. of (8).

(10) Sròn Garbh Choire (3250 feet)=the nose of the rough corrie. ¾ mile N.E. of (9).

(11) Meall an-t-Snaim (3180 feet)=smooth hill. 1 mile N.E. of (10).

(12) **Càrn Liath** (3298 feet)=the grey cairn. ¾ mile E. by S. of (11).

(13) A'Bhuidheanach (3177 feet)=the yellow ridge. ½ mile E.N.E. of (12).

(14) Stob Choire Dhuibh (3002 feet)=peak of the black corrie. 1¼ miles N.E. of (13).

The ridge runs on for another mile over the top of of Càrn

Dearg (2955 feet) and then gradually descends to the upper Spey valley.

Loch Laggan Hotel is the most convenient inn, and Tulloch is the nearest station.

The usual route for Creag Meaghaidh is from Craigbeg, half-way between Tulloch and Loch Laggan, up the Allt na h-Uamha (burn of the cave) and so on to the south-west slopes. A long but gentle ascent, mostly over grass, leads to the cairn.

Beinn a' Chaoruinn can be ascended from the same glen, or perhaps more conveniently from the direction of Roughbarn, 1½ miles from Tulloch Station. This mountain is a long, gently undulating ridge leading from the main top (two cairns) to the north top (no cairn). It passes over a slight rise in the middle, which was a top in the original Munro's Tables. From this rise falls to the east, into Coire na h-Uamha a fine narrow ridge which provides an easy and interesting route from the corrie. This ridge is conspicuous from the corrie and has a pinnacle near the foot.

At the head of Coire na h-Uamha is the ridge connecting Chaoruinn with Creag Meaghaidh. The Bealach a' Bharnish (2686 feet) is the lowest point.

The summit of **Creag Meaghaidh** is a great plateau sloping gently to the south. There is roughly 1 square mile above 3250 feet. To the north there is a line of steep ground and precipices, and near the edge of these, about 400 yards north-east of the cairn, is a gigantic cairn said to have been erected by a madman in memory of his wife. Five hundred feet below is Lochan Uaine, which drains into the Roy. One mile east are the fine cliffs of Coire Ardair, 1500 feet high, facing north-east. To the south and east the plateau runs out into three ridges, forming the tops (4), (5), and (7). The view from the top is not particularly good, but the Parallel Roads of Glen Roy are well seen, and Ben Nevis and the Aonachs show up well in the west.

A fine route for the descent is over **An Cearcallach** and down to Moy, about one mile from the south-west end of Loch Laggan.

There is rather a fine corrie between **Meall Coire Choille-rais** and Creag Mhòr, with cliffs about 700 feet high facing N.E. There appear to be three buttresses with two well-defined gullies. Due west of the lochan in this corrie a gully runs up for about 600 feet to the bealach between Creag Meaghaidh and Meall Coire Choille-rais. There is no cairn on this latter hill.

Puist Coire Ardair in the original Tables was called " Crags above Coire Ardair." The finest crags are actually farther north-west and due west of Lochan Coire Ardair.

Creag Mhòr on the one-inch map has its name about ½ mile south of the top. This is another instance of the name being applied to the point seen from the valley. The ridge continues E.N.E. past this top to Sròn a' Ghoire (? Windy Nose), which in the old Tables was a top with a height of 3150 feet. A steep descent can be made from here down to Aberarder and Loch Laggan.

The Window (3200 feet approx.) is a very obvious and conspicuous pass. It was probably used by Prince Charlie, who crossed it from the Lochiel country on 28th August 1746. A short distance to the east of where the Allt Coire Ardair passes under the Loch Laggan road, near Aberarder Farm, will be found a good path leading up towards the Window. The path keeps to the left bank of the stream and climbs steeply up the slopes to a height of about 1800 feet. It then contours round to the west and finally stops near the lochan at a height of 2046 feet, This path is a very convenient high road into the very centre of the Creag Meaghaidh group.

The eastern hills of the Creag Meaghaidh group are more commonplace than those already described.

From the Window an easy climb of 250 feet up grassy slopes places one on the first summit, **Poite Coire Ardair** (3460 feet). If one bears to the right on the ascent a scramble up broken rocks and boulders will be found. The top is the S.W. end of the 3250-foot contour and overlooks Loch Roy. The east top lies about ½ mile N.E. along the ridge, and from here very fine views can be had of the cliffs of Coire Ardair. These two tops were named in the original Tables " Creag an Lochain " and " Crom Leathad " respectively.

One mile along the ridge brings one to **Sròn Garbh Choire** (3250 feet). This top is the small 3250-foot contour on the one-inch map, about ½ mile S.E. of the name. To continue on the main ridge one must descend from here N.E. instead of following the ridge due east. Broad gentle slopes now lead over **Meall an-t-Snaim** (3180 feet) to **Càrn Liath** (3298 feet). The ridge now turns definitely N.E., and in ½ mile rises to the top, **A'Bhuidheanach** (3177 feet). About a mile farther on the ridge drops below the 3000-foot level to a broad bealach and then rises to the last top, **Stob Choire Dhuibh** (3002 feet). From here to reach Loch Laggan one should strike due south and so avoid the steep descent into Coire Dhuibh and the detour round Meall Ghoirleig. Alternatively the ridge can be followed ¾ mile to Carn Dubh (2955 feet) and then due east down to the path leading from Loch Laggan Hotel to the Corrieyairack road near Garva Bridge, which will be struck about the 1000-foot contour.

COIRE ARDAIR

This very fine corrie is situated on the eastern flank of Creag Meaghaidh. From Lochan Coire Ardair (2044 feet) the cliffs rise very steeply to the plateau level about 3500 feet. The cliffs run from Puist Coire Ardair (3591 feet) at first north-west to the gully north of the Pinnacle Buttress, then north past the main part of the cliffs, with the three buttresses separated by the three " Posts " or gullies for about 600 yards, and finally again north-west to the Window, with the cliffs gradually diminishing in height as the easy ground leading to the pass rises to meet them. The rocks are mica-schist, and the posts are evidently eroded trap dykes. The schistose rocks are very steep, but are broken up by grass-covered ledges. Most of the climbing is " vegetable," but here and there are stretches of clean rock.

The climbing is confined to three main divisions of the cliffs. First come the rocks of the Pinnacle Buttress, which are extremely steep. This is followed by the three Buttresses intersected by the three well-known " Posts " or gullies. Further to the north are the more broken-up rocks which have not yet been fully explored. These divisions are clearly shown in the photograph " Coire Ardair " (p. 129) and the diagram (Fig. 15).

THE PINNACLE BUTTRESS

This is bounded on the south by Raeburn's Gully, which has several easy pitches, but which makes quite a climb under hard winter conditions. It was first explored in October 1903 by H. Raeburn, H. and C. W. Walker, who also reached Raeburn's Ledge but which petered out. On the face above the gully are two intimidating narrow parallel gullies running straight up to the crest, shown in the diagram Fig. 15. These have not been climbed. Cutting across the face is a long horizontal ledge which was traversed in June 1937 by E. A. M. Wedderburn and J. H. B. Bell. It cuts the unclimbed gullies at above middle height, and from the ledge the upper parts of the gullies appeared climbable. The left-hand one of these parallel gullies does not continue right down to Raeburn's Gully. This ledge was named by its explorers Apollyon Ledge.

Further to the right the Pinnacle Buttress forms a distinct edge, and it was here that the first attempt to ascend the Pinnacle was made. In April 1896 Tough, Brown and Raeburn climbed out on to the edge from the Easy Gully to the north, but higher up traversed to the right below the steep finish and reached the Pinnacle by the short ridge which connects it with the plateau behind.

In June 1930 Bell and D. C. MacDonald climbed the Edge from the lowest rocks, where they found a good chimney. They also avoided the final steep section, but this steep finish was climbed in June 1939 by P. R. L. Heath and M. H. Cooke.

In May 1936 Bell and Wedderburn, starting from the lowest rocks not far from the innermost part of the Lochan, made a continuous but not direct route up the face to the left of the Edge, one of the largest and steepest mica-schist cliffs in the Highlands. Their route, Fig. 15 (g), lay towards a conspicuous red scar, and then to an upper chimney which they reached too far up to enter. They eventually reached the Edge below the steep final part. This is a long and interesting climb with several severe pitches.

THE ROCK FACE CONTAINING THE POSTS

This great wall of rock faces eastwards down the line of Coire Ardair. It is not so continuous as the steep front of Pinnacle Buttress, but it is more extensive and diversified. Of the 1500 feet of height from the lochan to the top of the cliffs fully a third if not more must be allowed for scree and easy rocks or grass at the bottom, and a winter view will show that the steepest and most continuous mass of cliff is to be found to the north of the Centre Post and above a long terrace which slopes upwards to the right from the easier slopes below the Posts. The three Posts are narrow, steep gullies formed by the erosion of trap dykes. This structure affords an alternation of very steep sections, sometimes over-hanging, with easy ones in between. The upper portions of the Posts flare out into funnels, mostly at an easier angle. The buttresses alongside and between the Posts share these characteristics to some extent and are built of schist.

A. Buttress.—This buttress was climbed in June 1906 by H. Raeburn and F. S. Goggs. They reached the buttress from the north from B. Buttress, crossing the foot of the South Post (*a*). The route then led up from ledge to ledge, very steep but not difficult, until a holdless pitch with no good anchorage was reached. A retreat was considered, but eventually a way was found to the left, and then curving back to the right the crest of the buttress was reached. Good clean rock led up about 50 feet to a traverse leading to the left to a fine, steep, narrow chimney. This gave out on a grassy shoulder, and the climb finished up some easy rocks on the right.

South Post.—An easy, wide gully leads up to a terrific pitch which has never been attempted. This commences at a much lower altitude than the great pitch in the Centre Post. In summer it is a long, almost vertical water slide with no means of escape on either side. There are other pitches above this on a smaller scale.

B. Buttress.—This has not been climbed from the foot, but in October 1903 Raeburn, H. and C. W. Walker traversed out of the Centre Post, below the great pot in this gully, on to the Buttress. From here they ascended to the top of the rocks by a route which became a ridge higher up, but involved a good deal of unsound rock.

Centre Post.—In April 1896 Tough, Brown and Raeburn were chased out of this by avalanches. In October 1903 Raeburn, H. and C. W. Walker reached a triple pitch above which was a great pot, running with water and filled with spray. They traversed out of the gully on to B. Buttress on the left, as stated above. No other attempts were made until C. M. Allan and J. H. B. Bell climbed to the great pot in hard snow conditions on 1st April 1934. They, too, retreated, as the bare ice wall behind the pot was manifestly impossible. A subsequent visit for inspection at the end of May revealed a great cauldron of spray with a stream pouring down the wall behind the pot at an angle of at least 70 degrees and disappearing into a tunnel beneath an old snow bed. The conclusion was that the Post was probably unclimbable in summer conditions.

They made another attempt on 21st March 1937, a day of hard frost with plenty of snow in the gully. At the basin below the great pitch a clinometer yielded a measurement of 55 degrees and on the wall behind the uniform angle exceeded 70 degrees. The height of the pitch could only be estimated as exceeding 150 feet. They cut their way across the wall and upwards to the right, the traverse of about 30 feet occupying one hour. Having regained hard snow they continued obliquely upwards to the right, then straight up and finally back to the left into the Post above the pitch. The final ascent went up a long, wide, shallow scoop of hard snow, leading to the plateau without any further obstacle by way of a cornice.

C. Buttress.—This has only been climbed by way of avoiding pitches in the bounding gullies the Centre Post and the North Post.

North Post is much narrower, hemmed in most of the way by steep walls of rock. It has never been attempted under snow conditions. On 21st June 1936 C. M. Allan, J. H. B. Bell, C. C. Gorrie and I. H. Ogilvie made an ascent, but were repeatedly obliged to pass the overhangs of the gully by climbing on the walls. The first of these " evasions " involved a sensational and severe lead by Allan up the left wall. Soon afterwards Allan and Ogilvie re-entered the gully, ascended it for about 100 feet to the base of another wall of rock which blocked it, part of which they ascended directly, but were ultimately forced to traverse a sloping grass ledge to the right. Good, steep rock followed to the top of the buttress on the right, and the climb ended on an easy ridge.

Bell and Gorrie continued up the buttress on the left, without re-entering the gully. The route involved several difficult pitches and developed into an *arête* which gave rapid but interesting climbing to the top, where it arched over to the right and joined the route followed by Allan and Ogilvie.

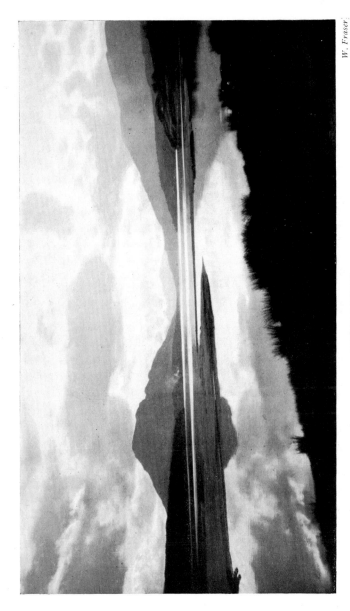

W. Fraser

LOCH LAGGAN

Binnein Shios, the distant Stob Coire Easain (Loch Treig) and Creag Meaghaidh.

GLEN BANCHOR IN THE MONADH LIADH

E. C. Thomson

COIRE ARDAIR

A. E. Robertson

THE CLIFFS OF COIRE ARDAIR, CREAG MEAGHAIDH

(see Fig. 15)

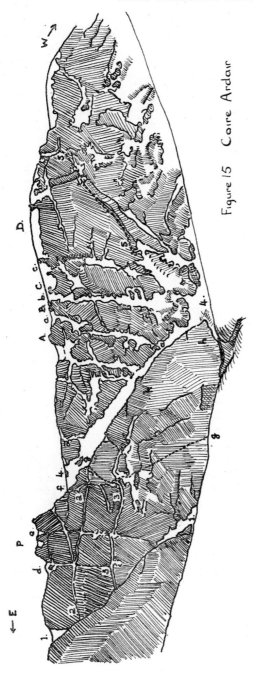

Figure 15   Coire Ardair

1. Raeburn's Gully.
2. Appolyon Ledge
3. Raeburn's Ledge.
4. Easy Gully.
5. Easy Terrace

A, B, C. The Three Buttresses.
   D   Creag Meaghaidh.
   E   Direction of Puist Coire Ardair.
   P   Pinnacle Buttress.
   W   Direction of Window.

a, b, c.   The Three Posts.
d, e.   Unclimbed Gullies.
f.   Unclimbed Gully near 1936 Route
g   1936 Route.
h   The Edge.

FIG. 15.—Coire Ardair

The end of the Post was found to be crowned by a huge, overhanging wall of rock, which had thus been circumvented on both sides.

THE ROCKS TO THE NORTH OF THE POSTS

Several shorter, but interesting and difficult climbs, have been made from the upper and more level part of the long, easy terrace which runs upwards to the right from the easier slopes below the Posts. The routes are none too easy to describe or differentiate. The first was made on 29th April 1934 by Allan, Bell, H. M. Kelly and H. Cooper. In snow conditions they ascended a short, difficult gully, just about the corner where there is an indentation and change of direction in the upper wall of rock. One difficult ice pitch was overcome. In January 1935 J. H. B. Bell and Miss V. Roy found this gully to be impossible and festooned with ice, but were able to ascend another close at hand by a difficult chimney, followed by much easier climbing to the top. On 4th April 1936 C. C. Gorrie and I. H. Ogilvie found the left-hand gully to be impracticable owing to loose ice. They ascended the *arête* on the right for 60 feet, but were forced to descend to snow on the right. This gully was also badly iced and the right wall was tackled. The gully could not be re-entered, and the climb was finished on this wall. It is unlikely that any of these routes can exceed 350 feet in height. The rocks do not appear to have been visited in summer, and this applies to the whole mass of rock between the North Post and the Window.

THE PASS OF CORRIEYAIRACK

(Coire Ghearr-eig, *i.e.*, the Corrie of the Short Notch).

In 1731 General Wade completed his new military road over the Pass of Corrieyairack (2543 feet) leading from Dalwhinnie and Laggan Bridge up the head-waters of the Spey to Melgarve and then northwards over the pass and down the Allt Lagan a' Bhainne and Glen Tarff to Fort Augustus on Loch Ness. In an old *Imperial Gazetteer of Scotland* there is a quotation from a traveller called Skrine who crossed the pass from north to south—in a *carriage*. He refers to the " inexpressibly arduous road . . . elevated to a height truly terrific—springing sometimes from point to point over alpine bridges and at other times pursuing narrow ridges of rock frightfully impending over tremendous precipices." Evidently a perfect paradise for rock-climbers ! As a matter of fact, the upper parts of the route are rather tame and uninteresting, being among scenery typical of the Monadh Liadth mountains. The approaches on both sides, however, are very attractive, and the views from the summit in clear weather exceptionally fine.

The road as constructed by General Wade left the Great North Road at Dalwhinnie and crossed over to the Spey valley near Laggan. It then ran up that valley, as already stated, and over to Fort Augustus. The portion from Melgarve northwards, about 13 miles, has been allowed to fall into disuse during the last hundred years. Most of the bridges are still standing and the line of the road can be followed easily nearly all the way. It is, of course, grass-grown, rocky, and in places more like the course of a hill burn, but it affords good going for the most part, compared with the desolate moor around it. The important bridge over the Allt Lagan a' Bhainne which had completely collapsed was renewed in 1932 by the Scottish Rights of Way Society.

The access to the stretch of road running up the right bank of the Spey from the main Loch Laggan road is not quite obvious. The original road was intended to branch off on the north side of the Spey at Laggan Bridge. From here the road curves round for 2 miles to recross the river by a large stone bridge which was, in fact, never completed and is now, of course, in ruins. There is, however, a foot-bridge across at this point. The correct route is to branch off the main road about ¾ mile west of Drumgask and join Wade's road near the ruined bridge. The road continues up the right bank of the Spey to Garva Bridge, where it crosses to the left bank about 8 miles from Laggan Bridge.

The carriage road ceases at Melgarve, about 4 miles beyond Garva Bridge. From here also a path runs up the valley west past Loch Spey (1142 feet), the source of the river, and over the col (1151 feet) leading to Glen Roy. As an indication of the level nature of this valley it may be noticed that there is only a rise of 165 feet between Garva Bridge and Loch Spey, a distance of about 8 miles. From Melgarve to Leichroy, in Glen Roy, is about 10 miles, and on this stretch the path is

sometimes non-existent.   After Leichroy it improves, and
the last 9 miles down Glen Roy is a carriage road.

The last 500 feet to the summit of the Pass is steep, and
here the road ascends by 12 zigzags.   At the cairn (2507 feet)
the route does not go down north into Coire na Cèire, but
continues on west, rising a few feet to 2543 and descends
by the Allt Coire Uchdachan to the new bridge over the Allt
Lagan a' Bhainne as stated above.   From the pass a short
climb of 400 feet leads to the top of Corrieyairack Hill
(2922 feet).

This route from the Great Glen to Speyside and the South
was always an important means of communication between
the Western Highlands and the South.   It was one of the
old drove routes, and Montrose is said to have crossed it in
January 1645 when marching to surprise and defeat the
Campbells at Inverlochy.   Prince Charlie used it in August
1745 to reach Dalwhinnie from Invergarry, and so avoided
General Cope's army which was marching on Inverness.

XXI

THE MONADH LIADTH

THE Monadh Liadth (Grey Moors) are situated wholly within the County of Inverness, and extend eastwards from the Corrieyairack Pass along the north side of the River Spey, forming the watershed between that river and the headwaters of the Tarff, Fechlin, Findhorn, and Dulnan. The highest part of the range lies between Geal-Chàrn, 3 miles N. by W. of Crathie in Laggan, and Càrn Sgùlain, 4½ miles N. by W. of Newtonmore. Within this area there are 8 distinct tops which rise above the 3000-foot contour line. From Càrn Sgùlain the range falls rapidly towards the east, and at the head of the Dulnan divides into two branches, the one running N.E. and N.N.E. between the valleys of the Findhorn and the Dulnan, the other continuing the E.N.E. trend of the main range and forming the watershed between the Dulnan and the Spey.

The following are the principal tops proceeding from west to east :—

Laggan Area—West of Glen Markie—

(1) Corrieyairack Hill (2922 feet)=Coire Ghearr-eig=the corrie of of the short notch. 1 mile N.E. of the Pass.
(2) Geal-Chàrn (2838 feet)=the white cairn. 1¼ miles S.E. of (1).
(3) Gairbeinn (2929 feet)=the rough hill. 1 mile E. by S. of (2).
(4) Meall na h-Aisre (2825 feet)=hill of the defile. 3½ miles N. of Garva Bridge.
(5) **Geal Chàrn** (3036 feet)=the white cairn. 3½ miles N.E. of Garva Bridge.
(6) Beinn Sgiath (2845 feet)=the wing hill. ¾ mile S.S.E. of (5).
(7) Càrn Odhar na Criche (2927 feet)=dun cairn of the march. 4 miles N.N.E. of (5).

North of Glen Banchor—

(8) **Càrn Bàn** (3087 feet)=the white hill. 2 miles E. of (7).
(9) Snechdach Slinnean (3011 feet)=the snowy shoulder-blade. ⅔ mile W.S.W. of (8).
(10) **Càrn Dearg**, N. top (3093 feet)=the red hill. ½ mile S.S.E. of (8).
(11) Càrn Dearg, S. top (3025 feet) ½ mile S. by E. of (10).
(12) **Càrn Ballach** (3020 feet)=cairn of the pass. 1 mile N.E. of (8).

(13) **Càrn Sgùlain** (3015 feet) = cairn of the basket. 2½ miles E. by N. of (12).

(14) **A'Chailleach** (3045 feet) = the old wife. 1 mile S. of (13) and 3½ miles N.N.W. of Newtonmore.

(15) Càrn an Fhreiceadain (2879 feet) = cairn of the watching. 3 miles N.E. of (14).

North and North-West of Loch Alvie—

(16) Geal-chàrn Mòr (2702 feet) = great white cairn. 3½ miles W. of Aviemore Station.

(17) Càrn Dearg Mòr (2337 feet) = great red cairn. 2 miles W. by N. of Aviemore Station.

(18) An Sguabach (2459 feet) = the brush. 1 mile S. of (16).

The eastern extremity of the spur that divides the Dulnan from the Spey, including Sguabach, Geal-chàrn Mòr, and Càrn Dearg Mòr, is composed of a reddish granite similar to that of the Cairngorms. The rest of the Monadh Liadth are formed of different varieties of quartz-schist, mica-schist, and gneiss, belonging to the series of metamorphic rocks that occupies the greater part of the Central Highlands.

Considering the extent of the range and the height attained by its central portion, the Monadh Liadh are, as a whole, singularly devoid of features of interest to the climber. They afford, however, fine moorland hill walks with extensive views of the Cairngorms and the mountains of Central Ross and Inverness. The summit of the range presents a wide undulating plateau covered with peat and fringe-moss on stony debris. On the north side peat-covered slopes descend in dreary monotony to the head-waters of the Fechlin and Findhorn, and the rock features are almost entirely confined to the corries and glens that fall southwards into Strathspey.

There are no recognised " climbs " in the district, and it would be difficult to make the ascent of any of the hills more than an ordinary hill-walk. Some fair rock-scrambling can, however, be obtained on the craggy faces in Glen Markie, Gleann Ballach, and the corries round Lochan a' Choire, east of Geal-Chàrn (No. 2) and Loch Dubh, south-west of Càrn Dearg.

Geal Chàrn (No. 5) and **Beinn na Sgiath.**—The north and south tops respectively of a bulky mountain on the west side of Glen Markie. A deep corrie with steepish rocks in places surrounds Lochan a' Choire, on the east side of the mountain. One of the numerous " windows " of this district

Uinneag a' Choire Lochain, is cut through the rocks at the head of this corrie.

The route is from Crathie up the west side of the Markie Burn by a good path. A slight dip separates the two tops, which are broad and mossy, or stony.

The nearest hotel is the Loch Laggan Hotel (7 miles).

The Red Burn, the head of the Markie Water, flows through a remarkable rock gorge with waterfalls, worthy of exploration.

Càrn Dearg.—This mountain forms a narrow spur projecting S.S.E. from the main ridge, and falling with abrupt and rocky sides into Gleann Ballach on the east and Coire Lochain Dubh on the west. A dip of about 160 feet separates the north end of Càrn Dearg from **Càrn Bàn** (old name, Carn Mairg), the highest point on the main plateau. On the east side of the hill is a small rocky corrie with finely glaciated dip slopes.

It is best ascended from Newtonmore up the Calder into Glen Banchor and thence up the east side of the Allt Fionndrigh for about 2 miles. Cross the burn and turn west over the peaty col N. of Creag Liath into the head of Gleann Ballach, whence an easy climb leads to the ridge between the N. top of Càrn Dearg and Càrn Bàn. From the summit cairn of the former the culminating point of the Monadh Liadth (3093 feet) precipitous rocks, among which grow clumps of the parsley fern, fall to the east into Gleann Ballach. The ridge can now be followed southwards to the second top (3025 feet) and the descent made into Glen Banchor at Dalballoch, and the road followed down to Newtonmore.

A'Chailleach (3045 feet).—A smooth-topped mountain 3½ miles N.N.W. of Newtonmore, with a fairly steep rock face on the east forming the cliffs of Coire na Caillich and Bruthach nan Easain (hillside of the waterfalls). One mile to the N. is **Càrn Sgùlain,** a mere stony eminence on the central ridge.

From Newtonmore the route goes up the Glen Banchor road and then N. up the Allt a' Chaoruinn for 1½ miles and then N.W. to the summit ridge.

Càrn Ballach, Càrn Odhar na Criche, Càrn an Fhreiceadain, and the lesser tops between the Dulnan and the Findhorn are featureless eminences, only slightly varied above the general level of the summit plateau.

Creag Dubh (2350 feet), the black crag, south-west of Newtonmore, forms an isolated hill cut off from the main plateau by the valley of the Calder. Though of no great height, this mountain is perhaps the most striking and interesting of all the Monadh Liadth. Its south-eastern flank presents an almost continuously steep rocky face, with fine vertical cliffs above Lochain Ovie at the southern end. The ordinary route follows the skyline from the farm of Beallid, but plenty of good rock-scrambling can be had on the precipitous face above the Laggan road.

Although of little interest to the climber, these hills have always been favoured by the ski-runner. Càrn Bàn, Càrn Sgùlain, and A'Chailleach have very suitable slopes for ski-ing, all within reasonable distance of Newtonmore and its hotels. The best run is probably from the summit of A'Chailleach south-east down past the Red Hut to the Allt a' Chaoruinn path.

It should be noted that an old drove road marked by cairns over the hills leads across the Monadh Liadth from Glen Markie to Whitebridge Inn on the Foyers river, Loch Ness. The route starts at Laggan Bridge and goes east to Crathie in Glen Markie and then north for about 3 miles up the Glen. It then ascends N.W. to Loch na Lairige (2500 feet) passing to the N.E. of Geal Chàrn, and descends by the east side of the Allt Crom to Sronlairig Lodge. From here a road leads down to the Fort Augustus road a little to the west of Whitebridge Inn. The total distance is about 22 miles.

INDEX

ADVICE TO HILL WALKERS

ADVICE TO HILL WALKERS

The Scottish Climbing Clubs consider it desirable to give advice to hill walkers—especially to those with limited knowledge of conditions in Scotland. The present time is appropriate as an increasing number of people make use of the Scottish mountains in summer and in winter.

The Clubs are constrained to give this advice owing to the accidents in recent years which led to serious injury or death, caused trouble and anxiety to local residents called from their ordinary vocations, and to experienced climbers summoned from long distances to render assistance. Such assistance must not be regarded as always available, and it is only fair and reasonable that local helpers be paid adequately for their assistance.

The guide books issued by the Scottish Mountaineering Club describe routes which range from difficult climbs to what are in fine weather mere walks. It cannot be stressed too strongly that an expedition, which in fine weather is simple, may cease to be so if the weather becomes bad or mist descends. In winter, conditions on the hills change—what in summer is a walk may become a mountaineering expedition.

In many cases accidents are caused by a combination of events, no one of which singly would have been serious. Ample time should be allowed for expeditions, especially when the route is unknown. Further, before setting out on an expedition, parties should leave information as to their objective and route and, without exception, have the courage to turn back when prudence so dictates.

In expeditions of any magnitude a party should consist of not less than three members, and they should never separate. If the party is large, two of the experienced members should bring up the rear.

If one member of the party is injured, another member should stay with him with all available food and spare clothing, while the remainder go to secure help. Great care should be taken in marking the spot where the injured man is left. Unless a conspicuous landmark is chosen, for example the junction of two streams, it is difficult to locate the spot, especially if the return is from a different direction or by night.

SOME COMMON CAUSES OF DIFFICULTY ARE :

Underestimate of time required for expedition.
Slow or untried companions or members who are in poor training.
Illness caused through unwise eating or drinking.

Extreme cold or exhaustion through severe conditions.

Poor soft snow ; steep hard snow ; snowstorms ; mist.
Change in temperature rapidly converting soft snow into ice—involving step cutting.
Rain making rock slippery or snow filling the holds when rock climbing.
Frost after snow or rain glazing rocks with ice.
Sudden spates rendering the crossing of burns dangerous or impossible and necessitating long detours.

[*Continued on next page*

HINTS—EQUIPMENT :
All parties should carry—
Simple First Aid equipment, torch, whistle, watch, 1 in. Ordnance Survey map, compass, and be able to use them.

Except in a few spots in Skye where the rocks are magnetic, the compass direction is certain to be correct even if it differs from one's sense of direction.

Ice axes should be carried if there is any chance of snow or ice and a rope unless it is certain not to be required.

CLOTHING : At all times reserve clothing should be carried. Temperatures change rapidly, especially at high levels. Clothing should be warm ; in winter a Balaclava helmet and thick woollen gloves should be carried. Well-nailed boots should always be worn.

FOOD : Each member of a party should carry his own food. Climbers will find from experience what kind of food suits their individual need. Normally, jams and sugar are better than meat as more rapidly converted into energy. Most people will find it advisable to avoid alcohols on the hills, but a flask may be carried for emergencies. Light meals at frequent intervals are better than heavy meals at long intervals. In winter it may be advisable to make an early stop for food if shelter is found.

It is essential at all times to respect proprietary and sporting rights, especially during the shooting season, and to avoid disturbing game in deer forests and grouse moors.

Issued with the authority of

Scottish Mountaineering Club
Dundee Rambling Club
Ladies' Scottish Climbing Club
Moray Mountaineering Club
Creagh Dhu Mountaineering Club
Edinburgh University Mountaineering Club
Cairngorm Club
Grampian Club
Lomond Mountaineering Club
Junior Mountaineering Club of Scotland
Etchachan Club

THE SOUTHERN HIGHLANDS

Edited by

J. D. B. WILSON, B.Sc.

including an Appendix on
the Rock Climbs in the Arrochar District
by

B. H. HUMBLE and J. B. NIMLIN

The area is relatively extensive. On the south bounded by the
Forth and Clyde Canal : on the east by the coast to the north side of
the Firth of Tay : and on the west by the indented coast north to
Oban, excluding the islands of the west. The peninsula of Kintyre is
included. The northern boundary follows the railway from Oban
east as far as Dalmally, then north-east by Glen Orchy to join the
West Highland line at Bridge of Orchy and north to Rannoch. The
boundary runs south-east from Kinloch Rannoch by the road to
Pitlochry then by the railway to Dunkeld, and to the Firth of Tay.

The book mentions all the most interesting mountains in the
region, and each chapter contains a note of recommended maps at
the beginning and a list of centres relative to the district at the end.
An endeavour has been made to obtain up-to-date and reliable information on paths and bridges. There is also an interesting summary of
the geology of the Southern Highlands by James Phemister, D.Sc.

Illustrated with **44 plates and one line diagram. Demy 8vo.,
xii + 204 pp. Cloth. Published at 15/- net.

THE WESTERN HIGHLANDS

BY

JAMES A. PARKER, B.Sc., M.Inst., C.E.

This book describes the mainland lying west of the Great Glen
and south of a line drawn from the Cromarty Firth along the valleys
of the rivers Connan, Bran, and Carron to the head of Loch Carron.
It is divided into ten districts and to each a separate chapter is devoted.

The district is of great interest to the mountaineer, and it has also
a strong appeal to the pedestrian. No fewer than 60 mountains exceed
3,000 feet in height. They are all described as well as many of the
lower.

It was the scene of the greater part of the wanderings of Prince
Charlie after the battle of Culloden. A short itinerary of these wanderings by the Rev. A. E. Robertson is included.

There are few public roads, but it is traversed in all directions by
right-of-way paths.

Third Edition, Revised. Illustrated with **28 plates and two
panoramas. Demy 8vo., viii + 136 pp. Cloth. Published
at 12/6 net.

▲ Indicates a Munro

1 2 3 4 5 6 7 8 mls.

Loch Lochy

Loch Arkaig

Parallel Roads

Spean Bridge

Loch Eil

Grey Corrie

Aonach's

FORT WILLIAM

Ben Nevis

Mamores

Aonach Eagach

Beinn Bheithir

Bidean nam Bian

Buachailles

Glen Creran

Clach Leathad

Loch Linnhe

Ben Starav

Stob Gabhar

Bridge of Orchy

Beinn Eunaich

Taynuilt

Oban

Cruachan

Dalmally